MATTERS OF
THE HEART

CHRIST FELLOWSHIP
CHERRYDALE

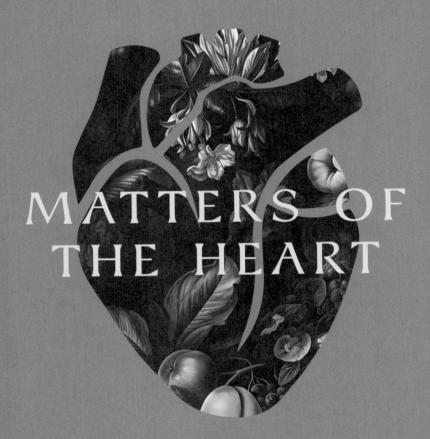

MATTERS OF
THE HEART

A 13-WEEK DEVOTIONAL
BASED ON THE BOOK
OF ECCLESIASTES

Matters of The Heart © Copyright 2023 Matt Rogers

Paperback: ISBN 979-8-218-30737-0

First Paperback edition December 2023

Written by Jacob and Laura Campbell, Leonard and Jessica Pisano, Matt Rogers, and Alyssa Trainer

Design by Sarah Dean

Edited by Micah Stewart and Tom Kline

Printed by Christ Fellowship Cherrydale in Greenville, SC, USA

Christ Fellowship Cherrydale, 401 State Park Rd, Greenville, SC 29609

www.cfcherrydale.com

MATTERS OF
THE HEART

A 13-WEEK DEVOTIONAL
BASED ON THE BOOK
OF ECCLESIASTES

CHRIST
FELLOWSHIP

TABLE OF CONTENTS

WHEN ALL HAS BEEN
HEARD, THE CONCLUSION
OF THE MATTER IS THIS:
FEAR GOD AND KEEP HIS
COMMANDS, BECAUSE
THIS IS FOR ALL
HUMANITY.

ECCL 12:13 CSB

INTRODUCTION

FROM MATT ROGERS

The best books about the Bible are <u>rooted</u> in vibrant ministry in the local church. In this context, pastors, leaders, and church members are best able to <u>see the needs of those seeking</u> to walk faithfully with Jesus Christ. The book you hold in your hands is one such example.

Christ Fellowship Cherrydale, located in Greenville, South Carolina, developed this resource to serve the church's members, and in turn, to serve anyone in the church at large who might benefit from thinking about the matters of the heart outlined in the pages that follow. Over the course of 2023, the church's preaching ministry worked through the books of 1 and 2 Samuel and 1 Kings, noting the rise and fall of the reigns of Saul, David, and Solomon. We ended the series at the culmination of Solomon's rule, just before the kingdom truly began to unravel. It seemed prudent to transition from Solomon's life to the book that functions much like his memoir—Ecclesiastes—which we worked through in the winter of 2024. Because the teaching series took place at the start of a new year, we recognized that many of our members would be attempting to re-engage spiritual disciplines like Bible reading, so we set out to write a simple devotional guide to accompany the teaching series. This devotional is not derived simply from the book of Ecclesiastes, however. We've taken the themes of each subsection of Ecclesiastes and developed daily readings from other Bible passages that address the same theme. Along the way, we've attempted to provide guiding questions that would help readers to meditate on the themes they are considering. The book is broken up into 13 weeks, with a unified topic for each week and 5 daily devotions to go along with the topic under consideration.

Not only is *Matters of the Heart* rooted in the church's preaching ministry, but it's also the work of various members of the church. Christ Fellowship has numerous thoughtful members who are passionate about the gospel and about God's word. We invited some of those members into the writing process—namely, Jessica and Leonard Pisano, Jacob and Laura Campbell, and Allysa Trainer. You will note at the beginning of each week who wrote that particular section, and we hope that the diversity of authors allows for more well-rounded engagement with the biblical text. Special thanks is also due to Micah Stewart and Tom Kline who helped edit and revise our writing.

It's our prayer that *Matters of the Heart* serves to equip our church and those in other churches to heed Solomon's wisdom to fear God and keep His commandments (Ecc. 12:13).

THERE IS AN OCCASION FOR EVERYTHING, AND A TIME FOR EVERY ACTIVITY UNDER HEAVEN.

ECCL 3:1 CSB

WEEK
01

Meaning

ECCLESIASTES
1:1–11

"ALL THINGS ARE WEARISOME, MORE THAN ANYONE CAN SAY. THE EYE IS NOT SATISFIED BY SEEING OR THE EAR FILLED WITH HEARING."

ECCLESIASTES 1:8

"HUMAN HISTORY IS THE LONG TERRIBLE STORY OF MAN TRYING TO FIND SOMETHING OTHER THAN GOD WHICH WILL MAKE HIM HAPPY."

C.S. LEWIS,
MERE CHRISTIANITY

DAY ONE

SCRIPTURE READING

2 Corinthians 4:7-18

"Absolute futility. Everything is futile" (Ecc. 1:2).

How's that for a New Year's message?

This time of year we are far more likely to scroll through topics exhorting us to take charge of our lives, conquer the mountain we've longed to climb, and make this year the year we finally break through the barriers keeping us from fulfillment.[1]

It is not likely that Solomon would be asked to write a blog for modern Americans entering a new year. And if he was asked to write, he wouldn't be invited back next year. But in some ways, this is what the book of Ecclesiastes is. It's a personal memoir from the richest, wisest, most important person to ever live. Its purpose is to dispel the notion that a fulfilling life can be found through worldly success. Throughout the book he simply holds up various

---

[1] This week's reflections are written by Matt Rogers, one of the pastors of Christ Fellowship Cherrydale in Greenville, South Carolina.

concepts that are thought to give life meaning, things like money or fame, and describes why they each come up short. He concludes that life under the sun is vain, which serves as the rationale for orienting life to something beyond the sun—to God and His purposes in human history.

For that reason, it's actually an ideal read for a new year. Like the people of Solomon's day, we are tempted to hyperfocus on the things that are right in front of us. We size up our life based on what we have, what we don't have, or what we want. We struggle to take our eyes off of what is here and orient ourselves to the unseen realities of God and his kingdom that transcends our little lives in our little world.

READ 2 CORINTHIANS 4:7-18. [2]

What do you observe about this passage?

Die to this world - and live!
Persevere by seeing the invisible!
↳ and living for..."

One thing we can say about the Apostle Paul is that the brother was honest. He told it like it is and never minced words about the pain and suffering he experienced in this life. I think he and Solomon would have been friends. They were both straight-shooters who got right to the point. Paul, in 2 Corinthians 4, describes a fairly miserable life. He's a broken jar who is afflicted, perplexed, persecuted, struck down. His

---

[2] We've intentionally chosen to not include the actual text of the Scripture here in this devotion. The aim of any good devotion is to press you into the Bible itself, so we thought you'd be best served by having your Bible open alongside this book so you can read and reflect on the passage we will ask you to consider each day. Unless otherwise indicated, the Scripture used in this book is taken from the Christian Standard Bible (CSB).

outer self is wasting away—a reality that is presumably true for both Paul and his band of missionaries, and for the early church.

In spite of this outward futility he is able to write that he is not crushed, despairing, forsaken, or destroyed. He does not lose heart. And, by extension, neither should others who are going through similar suffering in a broken world.

What is the basis for such hope? How can someone have such a positive outlook when things around them are so bleak?

The answer is given in verse 18—"we do not focus on what is seen, but on what is unseen." It seems that this statement is given by way of personal testimony (the Apostle Paul focuses on what is unseen) and by way of exhortation (Christians should focus on what is unseen). Notice the contrast. Paul states the obvious. The reason so many of us struggle to focus on what is unseen is because we get trapped in what is seen. And this makes sense, doesn't it? After all, what is seen is the world we inhabit. It's the daily realities that make up life. It's people and schedules and practices and dirty diapers and work to do and emails to send and looming frustrations and sickness and death. We see all of these realities vividly. And once we see them, we're prone to over-see them and hyperfocus on these realities such that we lose sight of a far bigger world that exists.

Beyond the concrete world that we can see lies the kingdom of God. God's kingdom includes our lives and the details therein, but it's far bigger than our lives. It's all of God's purposes and plans throughout all human history to bring about a renewed and restored world through the person and work of Jesus Christ. It's all that God is doing to bring that kingdom to bear on this earth as it is in heaven. It's the grand story of how God's plan from eternity past is coming to ful-

[handwritten in left margin: in "the Most H.ly Place." Heb. 10:19-20]

[handwritten in left margin: But we are invited to experience the presence of God]

[handwritten annotation: — and there may be others!]

fillment in and through our lives and our world. This realm is unseen, but it's no less real.

And if we focus there, our perspective changes. When we look at the kingdom, we see nothing but good news. We see evidence of hope amid despair. We see how God takes broken things and redeems them. We see his providential hand bringing about good from evil. We see how our prayers, our generosity, our love for him and his church is bringing about good in the world. By focusing on what is unseen, we are sent back into the world we can see with a different perspective.

SO LET'S START THERE.

Where are you most tempted to hyperfocus on things that you can see?

Meeting my physical needs + emotional needs for security in this world.

What is one aspect of God's often unseen kingdom that you can praise Him for today?

I am invited to enter in to "the Most Holy Place" now, not when I die, AND He promises to enter me. 1 Cor. 3:16

DAY TWO

SCRIPTURE READING
Matthew 6:19-24

Maybe you've watched a show about hoarders or doomsday planners. To some level, all of us make plans for the future. We might not plan at the level of those whose stories fill these shows, but our understanding of the future informs how we make decisions in the present. Some of this planning is sensible and wise—after all we need to care for ourselves and our families should we live to advanced age. Some of this planning is just over the top and consuming.

It is interesting that Jesus did not dissuade planning.

READ MATTHEW 6:19-24.

What do you notice about Jesus' challenge in this passage?

My security is not in or with the things of this world.

Jesus doesn't say that we should avoid storing up treasure. His challenge is that we need to be mindful of the location of that treasure. It's futile to store treasure on this earth because anything–thieves, moth, or rust–can destroy that treasure. This idea harkens back to our passage from this week from Ecclesiastes. Remember there Solomon tells us that life in this world is futile. By this he doesn't mean that anything and everything we do in this life is futile. It seems that the point is much like what Jesus says in Matthew 6. It's things done on this earth purely for life on this earth that are futile. It's putting good things, like our time, our money, our investment into gathering treasure in this life that is the problem.

Think about it this way—You inherit a really nice piece of furniture from a parent who recently passed away. It's handmade and has all sorts of memories of the life your loved one lived. You've got a treasure, and not just any treasure but a personal heirloom that's unique and irreplaceable. You're faced with a choice then. Where do you put it? You could take that treasure and put it out on the back deck between your other patio furniture. There it would sit out under the brutal sunshine day after day. It would be rain soaked, wind battered, and, before long, it would be destroyed. You could place the furniture in the kid's playroom. Would it fare better there? Probably not! There's another option. You could take the piece and put it in a place in your home away from traffic, a place where it would be seen and enjoyed but not destroyed, a place where the temperature and environment would be closely controlled and where the heirloom would have the best chance of being preserved.

I tend to read the language of "treasure" in Matthew 6 as referring to two distinct kinds of treasure, as if there is one kind of treasure on the earth and another kind in heaven. But that's not what Jesus says. He describes a singular treasure that can be stored in one of two distinct places. The same treasure. Different location.

In Matthew 6 he defines the treasure in the passage that follows. The treasure is money (v. 24). That treasure (money) can be stored on this earth or stored in heaven. In other words, money can be invested for earthly or heavenly purposes. I think it is fair to extend the notion of treasure to anything that humans possess. A treasure is certainly not less than money, but it's more. It's any quality that we possess that we can use or invest. Our time. Our gifts. Our emotional energy. Our service. While people possess this treasure to varying measures—some have more money, time, energy than others–God has given all people these types of treasure. It's then on that person to choose how they will spend what they've been given.

Notice finally that the choice is both ongoing and distinct. Ongoing in the fact that you do not merely choose once and for all where you are going to invest your treasure. It's a day by day, even moment by moment

decision. For many of you, perhaps you set up your retirement investment at some point and merely monitor the growth or decline of that
investment over time. You don't change it. It's on autopilot. The investment Jesus describes doesn't work like that. You don't set it and forget
it. You have to constantly go back, assess your investment, recommit to
having it in the right place, and make the daily decisions required to put
it in the right place.

And it's distinct. By this I mean there's no middle way. Either you
are storing up treasure on earth or you are storing treasure in heaven. You
don't get a third option and you can't do both. Jesus is clear—You can't
serve God and money. You have to pick.

So let's spend the rest of our time this morning taking inventory.

What treasure do you have right now?

Becky ... children + grandchildren

Financially secure

m)

**What evidence would you give that you
are storing that treasure in heaven?**

Serving in His name.

- Sacrifically?

- for His glory? or mine?

DAY THREE

SCRIPTURE READING
Psalm 1

The Wisdom books of the Old Testament (Job, Psalms, Proverbs, Ecclesiastes, Song of Solomon) are loaded with practical counsel for life. In fact, it would be appropriate to say that these books are nothing but practical wisdom—they give voice to the wise path for a full and meaningful life. Job gives counsel on how to relate to suffering and pain. The Psalms give insight for how to relate to God and understand His plans and purposes. Proverbs outlines how to relate to other people. Song of Solomon describes how to relate to a spouse. And Ecclesiastes describes how to relate to the world as a whole.

Since these books are grappling with similar topics, it would make sense for them to be interrelated. After all, understanding how to worship God from the Psalms helps me navigate suffering from Job. Or learning how to love my spouse in Song of Solomon helps me love other people that God puts in my life. In this way, I think Psalm 1 is a good front door into the house that Solomon builds in the book of Ecclesiastes.

READ PSALM 1.

What stands out to you about this passage?

If my mind is fixed on the things of this earth — I will not be happy.

Psalm 1 is both a warning and a promise. It's a warning to not follow the path of sinners, whose lives are like chaff that the wind drives away. It's also a promise. You can be like the one who is a tree planted by streams of water. You can live a fruitful life. You can prosper. Notice that this promise is not solely, or even primarily, about the afterlife. We aren't simply talking about eternity here. The Psalmist is reflecting on an actual life lived by a man or woman here on earth. This life can produce fruit that lasts.

If we're honest, the book of Ecclesiastes can feel like it's all warning and no promise. The tone of the book is bleak, some might say it's even pessimistic. I think a better perspective would be to say that the book is realistic. Solomon is real about the pain, the burden, vanity of life on this earth. It would be easy to wrestle with these concepts and conclude that there's just no point in it all. It's easy to become a nihilist if you spend too much time thinking about the futility of it all.

But that's not where the Bible wants to leave us. We aren't meant to walk away and throw up our hands in despair. Rather, we are meant to have a realistic appraisal of the world so that we can make wise choices about how we spend our lives. Far too often that which we think will bring peace and happiness, leaves us feeling lonely, isolated, and frustrated.

Loneliness. Alienation. Frustration.

Do you see it?

Do you feel it?

The fruit of our lives is often rotten. What's the alternative? Psalm 1 tells us. Fruitfulness is being a person who delights in the law of the Lord. In other words, a person who knows the Lord, loves the Lord, treasures the good news of God's love and care, and seeks to live in obedience to Him and His ways. The Psalmist uses a beautiful image to capture this reality—a tree planted right by a stream. The steady movement of water nourishes the tree and allows it to grow strong and healthy.

Perhaps you've seen a tree grow over time. When we first moved into our house some 10 years ago, our front yard was barren. I bought a sapling from a local nursery and planted it. Honestly, I wasn't expecting much. But now, after a decade of growth, I sit in the shade of this tree while I watch the kids play. It would have been impossible to notice the growth from day to day, but over time something remarkable has happened.

The same seems true for a life well-lived; a fruitful, meaningful life. It doesn't materialize overnight. Many days the growth isn't apparent, the fruit isn't there. Give it enough time, however, and something miraculous happens. This is the tension between Psalm 1 and the book of Ecclesiastes. Ecclesiastes warns of the shiny, glittery, sloppy pursuits that could cause us to take the tree of our life and plant it somewhere else. Psalm 1 reminds us where life is found. It calls us to meaningful stewardship of the life God has given and, as we are faithful to delight in the Lord, we find hope that a meaningful life can be found.

**Do you feel more depressed and apathetic
toward this life or optimistic and hopeful?**

Wavers between the two!

How might Psalm 1 bring you joy and hope today?

Re-center!

DAY FOUR

SCRIPTURE READING
Psalm 103

Mr. Realism, King Solomon, makes another honest observation in Ecclesiastes chapter 1: "The eye is not satisfied with seeing, nor the ear filled with hearing" (v. 7). Boy, ain't that the truth!

You've probably seen this reality play out in your own life. Satisfaction is hard to find, and it's even harder to find satisfaction in a way that truly lasts. We might land on something that provides a momentary blip of satisfaction, but given enough time, that sense of joy tends to fade. Take marriage for example. How common is it to see a couple who were once overjoyed in their engagement photos seemingly grimace at the mere mention of their spouse some ten years in? Or something as simple as that long-awaited vacation that you've been saving up for. It's great, but it's quickly a thing of the past only to be memorialized every year in social media photos

READ PSALM 103 WITH A UNIQUE FOCUS
ON THE FIRST SEVERAL VERSES.

What do you observe about satisfaction from this passage?

Satisfaction is from and in God

The Psalm begins with the writer talking to himself. Perhaps you've done this. You are sitting alone with a cup of coffee or out on a walk in the cool of the evening, and you are mulling over something that's frustrating about your life. You talk it out, attempting to find some answers to the various issues you face. You might even talk to God and invite His guidance and direction. Here the Psalmist talks to his soul—the innermost core of who he is. Three times he tells his soul to bless the Lord. How? Verse 2 provides the answer—"Forget not his benefits." We bless God when we call to mind the many benefits He provides.

That's a good place for a pause. In the Psalms you might notice on the right margin of various passages the term "selah." This word means a pause. It was likely a mark when these psalms were read or sung aloud. It was placed there to invite those reflecting on the truth of what's written to stop—to pause—and consider what they are saying. So Selah. How often do you call God's benefits to mind? Are you more often one who worries and frets about what might come in the future, or one who finds joy in what God has done for you already?

There's no word for "resume" in the Psalm, but imagine that we're now pressing our selah button again to resume after a pause. Once

you've had time to reflect on how well 14 you remember God's benefits, let's notice the two big benefits that this Psalm calls to mind.

First, the Psalmist reflects on the fact that his sins have been forgiv-
en. It's as if the Psalmist can't get over this idea:

- "He forgives all your iniquity; he heals all your diseases" (v. 3).

- "The Lord is compassionate and gracious, slow to anger and
  abounding in faithful love. He will not always accuse us or
  be angry forever" (v. 8-9).

- "He has not dealt with us as our sins deserve or repaid us according to
  our iniquities" (v. 10).

- "As far as the east is from the west, so far has he removed our
  transgressions from us" (v. 12).

One of God's benefits that we must not lose sight of is the fact that
Christians are forgiven of sin. All sin. Past. Present. Future. All forgiv-
en. Removed from our account. That's a huge benefit.

Then notice verse 5: "He satisfies you with good things; your youth
is renewed like the eagle" (v. 5). The Psalmist speaks of satisfaction
found in the good things that God gives. Most importantly, God is the
good thing. Satisfaction is found in knowing God.

And those who know God receive from God good things at His
will and discretion. I'd imagine you can itemize many of the good
things that God has given if you stop to think about it for a moment.
Sadly, it's common that we fail to recognize God's good gifts until they
are taken away. Once we lose something that we once held dear, we
appreciate how kind God had been in giving that very thing. What
would it look like for you to be more attentive to good things that come
from God?

We must learn to seek satisfaction in the good things that come from God and not the things that we think are good that we seek on this earth. If Solomon is right (and he is) and the things of this world are futile, then we can't look there for good things. This is a huge contrast—for example, do you find more satisfaction in the fact that your sins are forgiven or that you've seen growth in a retirement account? More satisfaction in God's presence than the prospect of finding a spouse?

We have to work to train ourselves to seek satisfaction in the right place.

Where are you looking for satisfaction right now?

Career

Financial Security

Running

Family Relationships

DAY FIVE

SCRIPTURE READING
Philippians 4:10-20

There's one final reflection in this first week that will get us moving in the right direction as we start the book of Ecclesiastes. Twice in the first 11 verses Solomon writes that there is "nothing new under the sun" (v. 9, 10). This will not be the last time he will say something similar. The language of "under the sun" is going to be common throughout the book. This is the place (under the sun) that Solomon will describe as futile and vain.

Let's fast forward to another Bible author considering the same

READ PHILIPPIANS 4:10-20.

What does God's Spirit call your attention to in this passage?

- Paul learned to be content in every circumstance
- Knowing that God would provide for him, to be able to deal with "much" or "little"
- God will meet our needs
- Our giving, that yields fruit, will be credited

There's a close connection between the satisfaction that we read about yesterday from Psalm 103 and the idea of contentment presented in this passage. Paul's life is hardly a model of ease or fulfillment. He's a needy and burdened traveling apostle who is dependent on the benevolence of God's people through the church. He's facing opposition on many levels. His solution to such a volatile life isn't found in appealing to God to change his circumstances. Rather he says, "I have learned to be content in whatever circumstances I find myself" (Phil 4:11). This is another "selah" moment isn't it. What would change about your experience of this world if you could echo Paul's claim here? What would it look like for you to be content in whatever circumstances you face?

I think it's instructive that Paul says that he has learned to be content. In other words, he didn't come into the world or into faith in Jesus as a full-formed, content individual. It took time and growth for him to get to the place where he could make such a claim. Now here is a place where we have to appreciate the normalness of Paul. Of course, he was a unique person who was used by God in a distinct way in the life of the early church. His role in spreading the gospel, however, should not cause us to lose sight of the fact that his character was not distinct. In other words, the virtues that we see Paul demonstrate were not only true of him, but were expectations and opportunities for all who follow Jesus. It's not just Paul who learned how to be content—we can too.

So take a little inventory right now and be honest. Use the scale below to indicate how content you feel in your life right now and use the space that follows to suggest why you would give yourself this score:

CONTENT   DISCONTENT

1   2   3   (4)   5   6   7   8   9   10

Why?

_____

_____

_____

Contentment has much in common with Solomon's conclusion about how to navigate a world that is futile. "Eat, drink and be merry" (8:15). In other words, don't try to expect too much from the world. Simply enjoy what you have and receive it from the Lord. Whether you have much or little (Phil. 4:12). Full or hungry (Phil. 4:12). Abundance or need (Phil. 4:12). This contentment is what Paul speaks of when he makes his famous claim—"I can do all things through Christ who strengthens me" (Phil. 4:13). We could substitute "I can be content in all things through Christ who strengthens me."

How does God teach us this level of contentment? You might think of the parallel to how a parent teaches a kid to swim or ride a bike. They progressively put the child in circumstances that challenge them, all the while standing beside them to catch them should they fall. In the same way, God teaches His children contentment by putting them in circumstances that are challenging and reassuring them with His presence. He's there—attentive and active to care for them in every circumstance.

It takes time for us to learn contentment because we have to have enough life experience to see God's care for us in different seasons and circumstances. We may intellectually affirm God's care, but until we've walked through various seasons (some good and some bad), it's difficult to have the resolute confidence that's required to be genuinely content, which is a key reason James (1:2-4) and Peter (1:6-8) are going to remind us that we should find joy in difficult times. Though the circumstances don't seem good, they are doing something good in us. And one of the greatest goods that comes through hard times is contentment.

What's something difficult that you've walked through lately?

Death of my son.

Moving - new home, job, church

How have you seen God use that to make you more content?

Not yet.

WEEK 02

Wisdom

ECCLESIASTES
1:12-18;
2:12-17

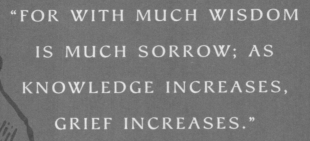

"FOR WITH MUCH WISDOM
IS MUCH SORROW; AS
KNOWLEDGE INCREASES,
GRIEF INCREASES."

ECCLESIASTES 1:8

"WE SPEND OUR LIVES LEARNING
MANY THINGS, ONLY TO DISCOVER
(AGAIN AND AGAIN) THAT MOST OF
WHAT WE'VE LEARNED IS EITHER WRONG
OR IRRELEVANT. A BIG PART OF OUR
MIND CAN HANDLE THIS; A SMALLER,
DEEPER PART CANNOT. AND IT'S THAT
SMALLER PART THAT MATTERS MORE,
BECAUSE THAT PART OF OUR MIND IS
WHO WE REALLY ARE (WHETHER WE
LIKE IT OR NOT)."

CHUCK KLOSTERMAN, *BUT WHAT IF WE'RE
WRONG? THINKING ABOUT THE PRESENT
AS IF IT WERE THE PAST*

DAY SIX

SCRIPTURE READING
1 Kings 3

It should come as no surprise to us that Solomon first considers how wisdom gives meaning to life—after all, he's the wisest person who ever lived. [3]For real. Read 1 Kings 3 and remind yourself of Solomon's background. What do you observe about this passage? What must it have been like to be Solomon?

[3] This week's reflections are written by Matt Rogers, one of the pastors of Christ Fellowship Cherrydale in Greenville, South Carolina.

_____

_____

_____

_____

_____

There's a certain eye-roll that's demanded any time someone tells you something that you are pretty sure they've never experienced:

- "Marriage isn't that tough", said by a couple 2 weeks into marriage;

- "Money isn't all it's cracked up to be", said by a single guy living with his parents;

- "Time will make the pain go away", said by a young pastor whose never counseled someone grieving the death of a loved one;

These claims might be well-meaning, but they fall flat if you aren't confident the person has enough experience to make the claim. Even if these less experienced people say something true, they are espousing something they've heard or think might be true, and not necessarily something they've experienced first-hand.

Throughout the book of Ecclesiastes, Solomon is going to make some rather large claims about this world. And we would be prone to write them off had they come from some nobody who'd never had money, never experienced pleasure, or lacked great wisdom. But when these truths come from the pen of the wisest person who's ever lived, we should sit up at the edge of our seat and listen intently. After all, it's not likely that any of us are going to have Solomon-like wisdom on our own. We should pay attention to what King Solomon has to say.

Where does Solomon's wisdom come from? The answer from 1 Kings 3 is clear—wisdom comes from God. Elsewhere Solomon writes, "For the Lord gives wisdom; from his mouth come knowledge and understanding" (Prov 2:6). This makes sense. God is the Creator of all things, and, as such, He knows everything about everything. He does not have to learn in order to be wise. He is wise, and has always been and will always be.

We know we need wisdom. Our lives are filled with all sorts of complexity, and the same is true for the lives of those around us. There's a seemingly unending maze of difficult decisions that we face.

The issue isn't whether we need wisdom, but where we look to find it. Everywhere you look, people are attempting to point you in the path of wisdom. There are podcasts, news articles, blogs on virtually every subject. Not to mention all of the "friends" of ours who give their wisdom freely on social media. Much of what purports to be wisdom is merely personal opinion, and much of it doesn't prove to be helpful in the long run.

Wisdom comes from God, and God is more than willing to give that wisdom to us as a gift. It's amazing to think that God—the fount of all wisdom—is willing to share that insight with us. He doesn't have to. He could merely store His wisdom in the heavens and leave us here to figure things out on our own. He could be like a 4-year-old on the playground and struggle to share what He possesses. Instead, He gives wisdom to others gratuitously.

We need Solomon-like wisdom that can come only from God. While we are not Solomon, we have access to the same God. And this God has declared His wisdom to us in the Bible. All Scripture is breathed out by God, the source of all wisdom (2 Timothy 3:16). In contrast to our impressions or sense of what God might be saying at any given moment, the Bible is an always truthful and clear guide for our lives.

God even saw fit to allow Solomon, the most wise person who ever lived, to write down some of that wisdom for us. Not only do we have the Old Testament history books that describe his life, but we have entire books like Proverbs and Ecclesiastes that are collections of his wisdom preserved for generations of Christians. We'd be foolish not to tap into this wisdom and use it to navigate our lives.

What about you?
Do you treat the Bible like it's a source of God's wisdom?

_____

_____

_____

_____

_____

_____

_____

_____

_____

_____

DAY SEVEN

SCRIPTURE READING
Proverbs 1:1-7

Most people would like to be wise. We might not be sure that we have the IQ to truly be smart, but we'd love to have the insight to navigate the complexities of life in a way that demonstrates that we are truly a wise person—regardless of how booksmart we may be. After all, sometimes there's a stigma associated with someone who is merely smart. We've even got pejorative terms like "smartypants" to refer to a person who is all brains and not much else. But a wise person is a gift, and we know it. When we walk through hard times, face a crisis, or have to make a difficult choice, we are looking for wise people to help us. Wisdom is a prized possession. We want it in others, and ideally we'd like to have it ourselves.

READ PROVERBS 1:1-7.

What stands out to you?

_____

_____

_____

_____

_____

In week 1 we mentioned that there is much in common between the books of Psalms, Proverbs, Ecclesiastes, Song of Solomon, and Job. They are classified together under the genre of Wisdom literature in the Bible. So it would make sense that the opening paragraph of the book of Proverbs grapples with the question of wisdom. Verses 1-7 ask and answer two important questions: 1) what makes a person wise? and 2) what does a wise person do?

What makes a person wise? This is where the passage ends in verse 7. Wisdom results from fearing the Lord. Said another way—if you want to be wise you have to fear the Lord. There's been much discussion about what it means, or doesn't mean, to fear the Lord. In this context, the fear of the Lord means submission to His authority. In other words, a person who fears the Lord is one who willingly, whole-heartedly submits to God's authority in his or her life.

We know this to be true in the imperfect world of families. There are unhealthy reasons for a child to fear a parent, such as in cases of abuse. But genuine love means that a child respects the authority of the parent to provide rules and instructions. Children who fear their parents in a healthy way know the parents are in charge, understand the rules they have put in place, see those rules as being for the child's good, and willingly submit to the parent's authority. Because the child knows what the parent expects, he or she makes decisions in light of what is honoring and pleasing to the parent's authority.

In the same way, wise people fear the Lord by coming under His authority. God has spoken and given clear rules and instructions that guide people into the good life He intends. So we fear God by knowing what He expects and living in light of those parameters. Like a wise child with loving parents, those who submit to God do so because they know that He knows best and His instructions are for their good.

Then, what do wise people do? Notice the list:

→ **They pursue righteousness, justice, and integrity (v. 3)**

→ **They teach their wisdom to the inexperienced (v. 4)**

→ **They listen and grow to know more (v. 5)**

→ **They seek out guidance (v. 5)**

In many ways this list is like the fruit that Jesus speaks of so often. It's outward evidence of an inward reality. Say you are wise, Proverbs says. Then prove it by pursuing justice, living with integrity, teaching others, and listening to wise counsel. Based on what we saw yesterday, Solomon is the perfect person to give this counsel since he's the human representation of God's wisdom. Notice how the four traits mentioned above would be useful to a king. Notice also how the fall of Saul, David, and Solomon can be traced to their failure to embody these traits.

In our lives, we often have to work from these outward fruit markers back to the root if we want to know whether or not we are wise.

We should ask ourselves if our lives are characterized by righteousness, justice, and integrity. Do we teach others to follow God's wisdom? Are we seeking God to know Him better? Do we seek guidance from others and genuinely consider what they tell us? The answers to these questions suggest whether or not we fear the Lord.

A good way for you to take a step forward today is to take one of these areas that you see the need to grow and do a bit of research. What does God say about righteousness or justice or integrity? What does He say about listening to others or seeking out guidance? A simple Google search or flip to the back of your Bible will likely point you in some good directions. So take a minute and look up God's wisdom on one of these areas that you know you need to grow in and write your observations in the space below.

WEEK TWO

DAY EIGHT

SCRIPTURE READING
James 3:13-18

What comes to your mind when you think of the word "wisdom"? You might have the image of the super-smart person who sat beside you in freshman chemistry and seemed to excel without any effort. Or you might think about some famous intellectual who has influenced knowledge with their insights.

Often, wisdom is equated with intellectual aptitude alone.

What do you notice about wisdom from this passage?

_____

_____

_____

_____

_____

_____

First, it's worth noticing how James connects wisdom to understanding. In other words, wisdom isn't merely theoretical. Wisdom is connected with real life insight—understanding of how the world works, what's truly important, and how one should live.

In verse 15, there is an unspiritual, earthly, demonic form of wisdom. We can discern wisdom that comes from below because it's rooted in envy, selfish ambition, disorder, and evil practice. In other words, James says, it doesn't matter how smart you are if your life is producing pain or chaos, or if you are merely living to please yourself.

In contrast, real wisdom is gentle, peace-loving, compliant, full of mercy, good fruits. Wisdom is unwavering and without pretense (v. 17). This kind of wisdom comes from above—it comes from God.

Notice the close connection between the fruit of wisdom and the fruit of the Spirit mentioned by Paul in Galatians 5:22-23. There he writes that the fruit of the Spirit is "love, joy, peace, patience, kindness, goodness, faithfulness, gentleness, and self-control." This connection is no accident, since true wisdom comes from God's Spirit.

Now we can work in reverse order.
Who is the most wise person you've ever known?

_____

_____

_____

_____

Odds are the names in that blank are not simply smart people. Rather they are those who have applied wisdom to live a distinctive life. They are wise because we looked up to them, we thought what they said mattered, we listened to them and followed their insight. I'd imagine that most of the names listed here are the kind of people who are loving, joyful, peaceful, gentle, and so on. These qualities allow us to say that a person is wise.

This is a far better definition of wisdom. We want to seek the Lord's help to become the kind of person who lives a distinctive, God-honoring life. We don't want to simply flex our intellectual muscles, but we want to grow in knowing God so that our lives produce the good works that God prepared for us to walk in (Ephesians 2:10). Find this type of distinctive life produced by God's Spirit and you've found a wise person, regardless of how smart this person might be.

This insight provides guidance for us as we think about stewarding the lives that God has given us. When we seek out God's wisdom from His word we need to do so with an aim for transformation. We do not want to merely acquire knowledge about God but we want to translate that knowledge into good works.

We know this to be true about other areas of life. It doesn't matter how much theory a person knows about computer programming, for example, if that person cannot translate this knowledge into practice. A company will not hire or promote on the basis of theoretical skill. They want actual knowledge that translates into business growth. Athletes don't sign contracts based on the concepts they understand in the film room, but on what they produce on the field.

Similarly Christians are called to do more than acquire knowledge. Of course, this knowledge is critical—after all, you can't obey a God you don't know. But we don't want to stop with knowledge alone. We want to translate knowledge into true wisdom that results in good works.

Do the marks of true wisdom listed in James 3 describe your life? Why or why not?

_____

_____

_____

_____

_____

_____

_____

_____

DAY NINE

SCRIPTURE READING
Proverbs 4:5-9

Why would God tell us to seek wisdom but also tell us that wisdom is limited? If you don't believe me, read Ecclesiastes 1:12-18 and 2:12-17 and compare these two passages with Proverbs 4:5-9.

What do you notice from this comparison?

_____

_____

_____

_____

You are going to notice this tension through the book of Ecclesiastes. Solomon is going to critique some things like money or work that are not inherently evil. Money is not bad, but it can be used in evil ways. Work certainly isn't bad—it was a part of God's original creation in the Garden (Gen. 2:15). But work is now infested with thorns and thistles, so it's got some inherent challenges (Gen. 3:17-18). The tension between something being good but not ultimate is at the heart of the book of Ecclesiastes.

We can multiply countless examples of this idea. Sports. Sports aren't bad; in fact, some could argue that there is much good that comes from a child playing sports. They learn discipline and teamwork. Sports keep them occupied, so they have less time to get in trouble in other ways. A child learns how to lose graciously through sports. All good things. But sports aren't ultimate. There's no use getting too bent out of shape about sports because one emergency is all it takes for the fun to be over. Even if you don't get hurt, over time you'll lose your edge and not be able to keep up. Sports come to an end.

Or consider marriage. Super good, right? A good marriage is a treasure, the closest approximation for God's love for His church. In marriage we find companionship, support, strength, and love. Not to mention the fact that marriage is the God-ordained way for having children and filling the earth with image-bearers (Gen. 1:28). But marriage isn't ultimate. Jesus Himself says, "for in the resurrection they will neither marry nor be given in marriage" (Matt. 22:30). Marriage can't be ultimate because it won't last forever. And even the best marriages come to an end on this earth, since most often one spouse dies before another. The temporary nature of marriage doesn't even account for the challenges that many marriages experience. Mixed within all the good of marriage are often many hard days as well.

Wisdom is like this. Solomon makes it clear in Ecclesiastes that wisdom isn't ultimate. The more wisdom you have, he writes, the more you know sorrows and grief (Ecc. 1:12-18). Even the most wise person dies and is forgotten (Ecc. 2:12-17).

But this doesn't mean that wisdom is bad. Much the opposite. In Proverbs 4, the same man who explained the limits of wisdom told his son to seek wisdom and get understanding as you might a fine treasure (Prov. 2:4). Twice in our passage today, he says clearly: "Get wisdom" (v. 5, 7). In verse 8, Solomon uses terms that would describe a couple in love. Cherish wisdom. Embrace wisdom.

He goes so far as to say that wisdom is supreme (v. 7). By this he obviously doesn't mean that wisdom is ultimate. Instead it's the supreme trait to seek out in this life. If you had to choose between money or power or pleasure, Solomon intends to encourage you to seek out wisdom above anything else.

Why should we treasure wisdom? Solomon gives us four reasons. First, wisdom will watch over you. Next, wisdom will guard you. Third, wisdom will exalt you. And finally, wisdom will honor you. Wisdom has a protective function. It oversees your life and keeps you from harm (watch over and guard). And wisdom provides value. It will lift you up (exalt and honor). Protection and direction. Guidance and value. Wisdom is a worthy pursuit, even if it's limited.

Do you pursue wisdom like a treasure?

Each day when your feet hit the floor, you will run hard after whatever you think the great treasure is. If the treasure, for you, is a life of ease and prosperity, then you will do all you can to make money and get ahead. If you think that the treasure is a well-run home with compliant children, then your daily decisions will flow from this goal. If you believe that health and fitness are the highest value, then you'll orient your life around your workouts and diet. We run after what we treasure.

Today's passage reminds us that wisdom is a treasure worth pursuing. In fact, it's a treasure of such value that it's worth giving up other, lesser pursuits in order to get wisdom. "Get wisdom—how much better it is than gold! And get understanding — it is preferable to silver" (Prov. 16:16).

Do you treasure God's wisdom and pursue it as you should?

DAY TEN

SCRIPTURE READING

Ephesians 5:15-21

The harder the circumstances, the more you need wisdom. I remember the day my father died in 2022. Within 20 minutes of getting the call from my mom that dad was gone, I was at their house and confronted with a day filled with more decisions than I'd made in most months. There was so much uncertainty and so many questions that needed answers quickly. Where would dad be buried? Where and when would the funeral take place? How would we pay for these things? Who needed to hear the news from me in a phone call? Who could I wait to tell later? How would we tell the kids? These questions are merely representative of the dozens of questions that seemed to hover over the room like pesky mosquitoes. As an only child, I knew that I had to lead and leading meant that I'd have to answer each of these questions wisely.

READ EPHESIANS 5:15-21.

What is the motive for walking wisely given in this passage?

_____

_____

_____

_____

_____

Paul says that the days are evil, so you need wisdom. Tough circumstances highlight the need for wisdom, and there are no tougher circumstances than living in a world broken by sin and Satan. The fact that sin has infested the world means that we are constantly going to need wisdom. The path the Lord intends for us to walk will be fraught with difficulty. There will be countless situations and circumstances where sin has so messed up a situation that it's hard to know what to do next.

In seminary we had to take a course called "Marriage and Family," and in that course we spent considerable time looking at God's word concerning topics like divorce and remarriage. For one assignment, we were asked to write our personal position statement on these issues, and I remember feeling a sense of smugness when I wrote my airtight biblical argument. The problem was that at that time I'd never pastored a church. I'd not sat in counseling offices or living room couches and seen the complexity of many marriages. I underestimated the reality of sin's impact. Now, this doesn't mean that God's word changed or that my personal views on divorce and remarriage shifted. But it humbled me when I started hearing the real stories of real sinners in a real world. There were, and are, many nuances to the wise step forward for a couple in crisis. They needed wisdom because sin's effects were clear.

The same can be said for all people all of the time in varying ways and degrees. Paul says that the days are evil (v. 15). To borrow an image from Jesus, the days are dark (Jn. 8:12). In the same way that you are more likely to fall down the steps at night, you are more likely to stumble when the days are dark. We must pay careful attention (v. 15) to how we walk. We have to have our eyes on the steps and consider the placement of each foot so we don't slip. Wisdom is our guide. It is our light. God's wisdom helps us see clearly in a dark world. Therefore, Paul writes, "don't be foolish, but understand what the Lord's will is" (Eph. 5:17). If we want to be wise, then we must seek to understand what the Lord says, what He wants, what He's called us to do.

The Holy Spirit is our guide for this type of wisdom, and He lives inside of God's people. In other words, we are not left to our own devices to attempt to find this wisdom. We can be filled with the Spirit, and He is the one who will lead us to all truth. Notice the comparison that Paul draws (v. 18). He says that we must not be drunk with wine, but instead be filled with the Spirit. The issue in both cases is control. Wine controls us and makes us do foolish things, or the Spirit controls us and leads us to be wise. Wise people submit themselves to the Holy Spirit's control. Can that be said of you?

If not, if you are controlled by anything other than God, you are in for a challenge in this life. Remember, the days are evil. The prince of the power of the air, the spirit that is at work in the sons of disobedience, Satan himself is at work all around us (Eph. 2:1-3). This side of heaven, the impact of sin will continue to make the days difficult and the need for wisdom clear. So start this day giving yourself to the Spirit's control.

You might do this through prayer, asking God the Spirit to make you wise and submissive to His leadership today. That's a great way to start every day because every day we face the temptation to submit to other, lesser gods. You might seek the Spirit's help through the Word. Reflect on this passage from Ephesians 5 throughout the day. Maybe write it on a notecard or screenshot it to your phone so you will see it throughout the day. Another biblical way to train yourself to submit to the Holy Spirit's control is through fasting. Refraining from food for a meal, a day, or a few days, can be a great way to help you see your need to be led by God and not by your appetites.

What is one way you can seek to give God control of your life today?

_____

_____

_____

_____

_____

_____

_____

_____

_____

_____

WEEK
03

Pleasure

ECCLESIASTES
2:1-3; 6:1-12

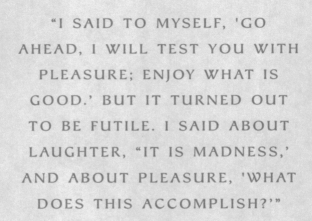

"I SAID TO MYSELF, 'GO
AHEAD, I WILL TEST YOU WITH
PLEASURE; ENJOY WHAT IS
GOOD.' BUT IT TURNED OUT
TO BE FUTILE. I SAID ABOUT
LAUGHTER, "IT IS MADNESS,'
AND ABOUT PLEASURE, 'WHAT
DOES THIS ACCOMPLISH?'"

ECCLESIASTES 1:8

"What is painful in pleasure? It is that in
all pleasure a person desires eternity, but
knows that pleasure is transient and will
end. That is not a knowing that comes from
a prior knowledge now applied to every
pleasurable event; it is something that the
depth of pleasure itself discloses to us if we
listen to it: a thirst, a craving, for eternity,
precisely because pleasure is not eternal but
instead has fallen prey to death. because
pleasure is not eternal but instead has
fallen prey to death."

DIETRICH BONHOEFFER,
CREATION AND FALL

DAY ELEVEN

SCRIPTURE READING

Psalm 16

After Solomon realizes the emptiness of life when wisdom is ultimate, he moves on to explore pleasure: "I said to myself, 'Go ahead, I will test you with pleasure; enjoy what is good.' But it turned out to be futile" (Ecc. 2:1).⁴ You can almost imagine Solomon looking at a lineup of money, power, pleasure, and the like and going one by one down the line to see if any of these things will satisfy the human heart.

Think back to a moment in your life that you deeply looked forward to. It could be a day such as Christmas or a birthday. Maybe it was an event like a wedding or the birth of a child. Or a big football game or concert. As you think about this moment or event, remember the excitement and anticipation you had. Maybe you couldn't sleep the night before, or you couldn't focus on your

This week's reflections are written by Jacob Campbell, a member of Christ Fellowship Cherrydale in Greenville, South Carolina.

work in the weeks leading up to that event. You knew that you would experience great pleasure when the day rolled around.

As a human race, we have an innate desire for pleasure and comfort. We long to experience beauty and avoid pain. It is for this reason that we anxiously await days that promise pleasure. Unfortunately, we live in a broken world marred by sin and death. These moments of pleasure are fleeting and fickle—leaving us feeling hollow and empty in the aftermath. These feelings are what Solomon references as he writes about the futility of pleasure. We are left in an uncomfortable spot. If pleasure is fleeting and meaningless, where can we find our joy?

David has some helpful pointers for us in Psalm 16. What does David mean when he says that eternal pleasure is at the right hand of God? How does this truth bring you comfort?

_____

_____

_____

_____

_____

David reminds us that we have something more to look forward to and anticipate. We have a pleasure awaiting us in eternity with our heavenly Father. It is important to distinguish the pleasure that the Psalmist describes from the pleasure that Solomon laments. Revelation 21 tells us that in the new heavens and the new earth God will dwell with mankind. The pleasure that we will experience in heaven is not due to worldly comforts or fading luxuries, but instead comes from being in the presence of the Creator of the universe. We will experience the perfect unity that existed between God and man in the Garden before sin stained that relationship. What an incredible promise for the believer!

This still leaves us with a question, "How do we live this life before the pleasure that heaven promises?" David's declaration is that the Lord makes known the path of life. The Lord will be faithful to direct our path. He knit us together in our mother's womb (Ps. 139:13) and has predestined good works for us to walk in (Eph. 2:10). Because of this, we can trust him to lead us, and we must be obedient to follow him.

Obeying and following Jesus does not often equate to experiencing pleasure or comfort in this life. More often than not, it requires us to embrace hardship and suffering. However, following Jesus provides meaning to the futile life that Solomon wrestles with. The Lord wants the whole world to be filled with the knowledge of His Glory like the water covers the sea (Hab. 2:14), and God has invited us to invest with Him in this process. We have the privilege of stepping into the dark and broken world in which we live and proclaiming the promises of a future pleasure that is eternal and will never fade.

In his book The Last Battle, C.S. Lewis' description of heaven should encourage us to press on through the futility of this life. There he writes:

> "But for them it was only the beginning of the real story. All their life in this world and all their adventures in Narnia had only been the cover and the title page: now at last they were beginning Chapter One of the Great Story, which no one on earth has read: which goes on forever: in which every chapter is better than the one before."

Praise the Lord that this life is only the title page and that we have a story to look forward to that will only get better.

How does the hope of eternal pleasure in unity with the Father prompt you to live differently this week?

_____

_____

_____

_____

_____

_____

_____

_____

_____

_____

_____

_____

_____

_____

_____

_____

_____

_____

DAY TWELVE

SCRIPTURE READING

Titus 3:3-7

The allure and desire of pleasure tugs at the human heart. This desire leads Solomon to find meaning and life in pleasure. Pleasure in and of itself is not evil. Like everything in this world, pleasure was created by God as a gift. Unfortunately, like everything in this world, that gift has been corrupted by sin.

A quick look back at Solomon's life shows us that he was no stranger to pleasure. He was the King of the most powerful nation of his time. He lived in a massive palace with servants to do whatever he asked of them. He had all the riches in the world and could purchase anything he wanted. Despite all of this, he writes "God gives a person riches, wealth, and honor so that he lacks nothing of all he desires for himself, but God does not allow him to enjoy them" (Ecc. 6:2). Solomon's declaration that there is no joy to be-found in the pleasure he has amassed for himself is sobering. No matter what, pleasure will overpromise and underdeliver.

READ TITUS 3:3.

What is a passion or pleasure that you feel enslaved by at the moment?

_____

_____

_____

_____

In many of Paul's letters, he summarizes our nature apart from Christ using the phrase "the flesh." "The flesh" doesn't refer to a physical body alone, but our nature that is enslaved by sin. It is a reference to our fallen state as sinners.

Our sinful flesh takes what was created for blessing and corrupts it. The flesh takes God's blessings and uses them for selfish pleasure. Notice that Paul describes our lives before salvation as being enslaved by passions and pleasures. This brings up the question that if pleasure was created as a blessing, how does it turn into something that enslaves us?

The answer to that question can be found in the way that we view pleasure. Pleasure has the power to enslave when it is the object of our worship instead of the vehicle for our worship. Our flesh pushes us to worship pleasure. To run after the next adventure or high. It leads us to view pleasure as an emotion that will comfort us in the pain that accompanies the broken world that we live in. Worshiping pleasure can take many different forms. There is a temptation to look at the lavish lifestyle Solomon lived and excuse our own sin because we are not engaging in the overflow of our riches like he was. We must push against this way of thinking and realize that worshiping pleasure can be as simple as watching a Netflix show. In our attempt to find meaning in life, we overindulge ourselves in the world. But the pleasure from a Netflix show eventually dies out, and we are left searching for pleasure yet again. We are in need of something more. We are in need of a Healer who can do more than numb our pain.

READ TITUS 3:4-7.

How does God's kindness affect
the broken desires of our flesh?

_____

_____

_____

_____

_____

Paul beautifully contrasts a life lived in the flesh where we chase pleasure as a numbing agent, to a life lived in the Spirit where we are regenerated by His Spirit and made heirs to the Kingdom. Because of God's kindness in sending His Son to bear the brokenness of the world, we have fulfillment in Christ and no longer need to run after worldly pleasure.

Look at verses 5 and 6 specifically. God saved us from the passions and pleasures of the world, not because of anything we had done. By saving us, He poured out His Spirit on us. Notice the adjective that describes how He gives us His Spirit. Depending on your translation, it says *abundantly* or *richly* or *generously*. Instead of looking for meaning in an abundant life of pleasure and passion, we have been given an abundance of the Holy Spirit to accompany us and to help us engage the broken world we find ourselves in. Where pleasure overpromises and underdelivers, God promises and completely delivers.

While we may not have the pleasures Solomon enjoyed to the same extent, we do have the same temptation to worship our flesh. Christians don't live without pleasure, rather, they seek to kill the flesh through the power of God's Spirit and find greater pleasure through worshiping the God who made all pleasure. They then find that this worship makes all pleasures of this life secondary at best.

> Where are you tempted to worship pleasure right now, and
> how might Jesus be inviting you to rely on the abundant
> outpouring of his Spirit?

DAY THIRTEEN

"Don't throw the baby out with the bathwater" seems to be a pertinent saying for our discussion of pleasure. There is a tendency for us to read Solomon's teachings and deduce that in order to follow Jesus, we must live a life of asceticism and deny ourselves any form of pleasure. Because pleasure is sin, right?

This is a common overcorrection that can prove costly. As we discussed yesterday, pleasure was created for us as a gift and as an avenue to commune with our heavenly Father. Solomon's search for meaning in pleasure comes up empty because he wanted pleasure to accomplish something it was never created to accomplish. Pleasure was never supposed to be the object of our worship. Instead, it was created as a vehicle for our worship. Rather than denying ourselves pleasure in order to pursue righteousness, let's

MATTERS OF THE HEART

reframe our view of pleasure in order to deepen our relationship with Jesus. This is obviously easier said than done. found in the pleasure he has amassed for himself is sobering. No matter what, pleasure will over-promise and underdeliver.

How can pleasure lead us to worship our Creator more intimately?

READ PSALM 37:1-7

**How does David contrast Godly pleasure
and worldly pleasure?**

_____

_____

_____

_____

_____

David begins Psalm 37 by reminding us to pay no attention to those in the world and their accomplishments. It is easy for us to be enticed by the world and long for the perceived pleasure that those in the world experience. Instead David exhorts us to trust and delight ourselves in the Lord. This is followed by a promise: if we do this, He will give us the desires of our heart. As our trust is placed in the Lord and our worship is directed toward Him, our desires become aligned with His. The pleasure of the world becomes less appealing compared to the wonderful communion we experience with Jesus. The desires of our hearts are changed to reflect the desires of Jesus' heart.

If our desires are aligned with God's desires, we can find pleasure in the things that God finds pleasure in. We see God take pleasure in a plethora of things throughout Scripture. He takes pleasure in His creation when He declares it good and walks in the garden in the cool of the day with Adam and Eve (Gen. 1-2). He takes pleasure in making known to us the mystery of His will (Eph. 1:9). He takes pleasure in His Son (Lk. 3:22). The fact that God takes pleasure in His Son is incredible news for us who are in Christ. Because of what Jesus did on the cross, we have been given His righteousness and are now also seen as sons and daughters. We can thus live in the truth that God takes pleasure in us.

If God takes pleasure in us and our desires are slowly being aligned with His, experiencing pleasure in this world is not something we must run from, but is something that can help orient our hearts to worship the Creator.

Think about the pleasure that accompanies the rising sun on a quiet morning or the unbridled joy that you experience when a child is born. Maybe it's the enjoyment of a perfect bite of steak or the embrace of a loved one after being apart for a long time. Pleasure lives in all of these moments. When we let pleasure be a vehicle for our worship, these moments bring our attention to our Creator. They posture our hearts to cry out for joy because of His kindness to us. They remind us that despite the broken world that we live in, we have a Father who delights in us and wants to give us the desires of our hearts.

Pleasure isn't the enemy. We aren't monastics, attempting to make ourselves as miserable as possible in order to show God that we are serious about Him. We aren't trying to deaden pleasure so we sleepwalk through life. You've probably met people like this. Sadly it's common to meet Christians who seem to be perpetually on edge and unhappy. That's not the goal.

We want to fully enjoy life by refraining from worshiping pleasure and directing our pleasures to their source by worshiping God. We want to take delight in God, who is the source of all the things that bring us delight in this world.

What could you change in your day to day life to allow
pleasure to become a vehicle for you to worship?

_____

_____

_____

_____

_____

_____

_____

_____

_____

_____

_____

_____

_____

_____

DAY FOURTEEN

SCRIPTURE READING
Philippians 3:1-11

Yesterday we discussed the beauty of pleasure and how it can lead our hearts to worship. Today we will consider the antithesis of pleasure: suffering and how it also can bring our hearts to a place of dependence and worship. Suffering and pleasure have a unique relationship. While our human nature pushes us to pursue pleasure and comfort and to avoid suffering at all costs, we are faced with the uncomfortable truth that the Bible talks about suffering as an unavoidable and expected reality of our walk with Jesus. Solomon lived a life filled with comfort and pleasure, and still his heart turned from the Lord to other gods. When pleasure is viewed incorrectly, it can lead us to look for comfort in the world and to rely on ourselves for happiness. The Lord uses our experiences of suffering to reorient our gaze on Him as we walk through this broken worl

READ PHILIPPIANS 3:1-11.

What does Paul say about suffering in this passage?

_____

_____

_____

_____

_____

Notice Paul's usage of "the flesh" in the beginning verses of this chapter. Once again we see this reminder that the flesh is deadly. Paul exhorts the Phillipian church to avoid putting confidence in the flesh (Phil. 3:4).

He then goes on to discuss his "fleshly" credentials. Paul had it made in the Jewish culture of the time—He was at the top of the food chain. He was a part of the religious elite and would have lived a very privileged and pleasurable lifestyle. He was living the dream of many young Jewish boys at the time. Yet he says, "I also consider everything to be a loss in view of the surpassing value of knowing Christ Jesus my Lord" (Phil. 3:8). Paul concludes this thought by stating that because nothing else satisfies, his goal is to know Jesus in the "power of his resurrection and the fellowship of his sufferings, being conformed to his death" (Phil. 3:11). Paul powerfully declares that he will gladly trade the pleasures of life for the privilege of knowing Christ and sharing in his suffering. This verse leaves the question for us to answer: How can suffering be a privilege?

Paul paints a picture for us of suffering as a means of relationship. In the chapter right before this, Paul talks about how Jesus gave up the comfort and pleasure of heaven and a perfect relationship with the Father—humbling himself by becoming obedient to death on a cross (Phil. 2:4-8). Jesus suffered the loss of everything and thus is acquainted with Paul's suffering.

This pattern holds true for us as well. Suffering provides an opportunity for us to know Jesus more deeply because we get a small taste of the suffering he experienced. He wants to know us in those spaces and invites us into a deeper relationship with Him because He is acquainted with suffering. This requires faith on our part. God also uses suffering to break our hold on the fleeting pleasures of this life and redirect our attention to Him.

We are prone to ask why God would allow us to suffer. Suffering is painful and often does not make sense. Unfortunately, God does not promise to ever answer this question. The question we need to ask is: Where are you God? This question facilitates relationship and relies on God to hold true to His promise to be with us always (Mat. 28:20). God does not promise that He will withhold suffering from His people. He instead promises that He will walk through suffering with His people as He invites them to know Him more deeply.

Our human nature tells us to run from pain and suffering and pursue pleasure and comfort. Solomon is an example of a man who did pursue pleasure and was not able to find fulfillment. It ultimately made him complacent. We contrast Solomon with the example of Paul, who turned his back on fleeting pleasure and embraced suffering in order to know God more intimately. We are called to do the same. Suffering is a gift from God to help us fight the complacency that pleasure and comfort foster in our hearts. Suffering, when seen through the lens of relationship, is an opportunity to know God more intimately. Suffering is not forever. We have a promise that one day sin will no longer exist and we will live in perfect unity with the Father. On that day, we will not need suffering in order to know God more intimately because we will already be living in perfect relationship with Him. Let us hold on to the tension of "already but not yet" as we suffer in this broken world while holding onto our future hope.

What is a current suffering or trail that you are experiencing?
How is God inviting you into a deeper relationship
with Him in the midst of it?

_____

_____

_____

_____

_____

_____

_____

_____

_____

_____

_____

_____

_____

DAY FIFTEEN

SCRIPTURE READING
Revelation 21:1-7

We can hear Solomon's exasperation when he says "For who knows what is good for anyone in life, in the few days of his futile life that he spends like a shadow? Who can tell anyone what will happen after him under the sun" (Ecc. 6:12). There is little hope in Solomon's voice as he concludes his writing on pleasure.

We are faced with a similar temptation as we come to the end of this conversation. As we concluded in our earlier discussions this week, our flesh makes interacting with pleasure very difficult and constantly tempts our hearts to worship pleasure instead of allowing pleasure to direct our hearts to worship our Creator.

But we do not have to despair in our flesh because there is good news for us. Christ has conquered the flesh and given us His Spirit to help us renew our minds in this broken world. He has also promised a day when the flesh will be no more, and we will be restored to perfect unity with the Father. This is the hope we have in Christ, that because of His death and resurrection, we can experience pleasure on this earth as a foretaste of that glorious day to come.

READ REVELATION 21:1-7.

What emotions does this passage invoke in you?

_____

_____

_____

_____

_____

_____

John beautifully describes a world where God's presence perfectly dwells with man. A world where tears, pain and death no longer exist. A world that is perfect and without sin. Notice in verse 5 God declares "Look, I am making all things new"(Rev. 21:6). What an incredible promise to the believer. There will come a day when the sin-stained world we live in will be made completely new. The brokenness that we wrestle with every day will no longer be present, and we will be restored to perfect unity with our Creator.

The idea of a coming wholeness applies to pleasure. In the new heavens and the new earth, pleasure will be made new. We will no longer have to wrestle with our sinful heart's desire to worship pleasure. Instead, pleasure will be a powerful vehicle for worship of our Creator and Sustainer for eternity. We will no longer need to guard our hearts against the pleasures of the world, but will be able to fully give our hearts over to the pleasure that comes from being united with the Father.

God goes on to command John to "write because these words are faithful and true" (Rev. 21:6). This is a powerful picture of God using John to communicate the hope of eternity. It's as if God knew that we would have a tendency to get lost in the futility of this broken world. His words are faithful and true. We are able to hope in the promises and perfection that heaven offers. God in His kindness has also allowed pleasure to be a vehicle by which we are provided a glimpse of heaven. We have an opportunity to pause in these moments and to let our hearts reflect on the hope that pleasure offers. These moments were never meant to last. God uses their fleeting nature to awaken our hearts to action.

When Jesus showed up on the scene, He declared that the Kingdom of Heaven was at hand (Mat. 3:2). Let us use these moments of pleasure that we experience as a catalyst to participate in the work of the Kingdom right now. This is the answer to Solomon's earlier question about life's futility. God has already begun the process of renewing this world, and we have an opportunity to participate in this process with Him. This gives our life meaning and purpose and allows us to have hope for the future.

As we walk with hope into the coming day, let us speak boldly of the current pleasure that can be had in knowing Jesus, and of the future, eternal pleasures at the right hand of the Father.

Pray that the Lord would bring to mind one person that needs to hear of the future pleasure that heaven promises. Who is this person?

_____

_____

_____

_____

_____

_____

_____

_____

_____

_____

_____

_____

_____

_____

_____

_____

_____

WEEK
04

Possessions

ECCLESIASTES
2:4-11; 4:4-16;
5:8-20

"THE ONE WHO LOVES
SILVER IS NEVER SATISFIED
WITH SILVER, AND WHOEVER
LOVES WEALTH IS NEVER
SATISFIED WITH INCOME. THIS
TOO IS FUTILE. WHEN GOOD
THINGS INCREASE, THE ONES
WHO CONSUME THEM MULTIPLY;
WHAT, THEN, IS THE PROFIT TO
THE OWNER, EXCEPT TO GAZE
AT THEM WITH HIS EYES?"

ECCLESIASTES 5:10-11

"A GREAT FORTUNE IS A
GREAT SLAVERY."

SENCA,
CONSOLATION TO POLYBIUS

DAY SIXTEEN

SCRIPTURE READING
Luke 12:13-21

Money can't buy happiness.

...but it can buy ice cream, a new phone, fresh sneakers, good food, gifts for loved ones, sometimes even the love or approval of others. So it basically can buy happiness. Right?[5]

In Solomon's case, money bought houses and vineyards, gardens and parks, fruit trees and forests, pools, servants, jewels, personal musicians—every comfort, whatever he desired, was his (Ecc. 2:4-10). Wouldn't that be nice? Even aside from luxuries, there is a sense of security in knowing that we can pay for what we need and for what we want. And it is not evil to have money or possessions! We need money to live, and God is gracious to provide it.

So, what does King Solomon —the one who held nothing back from himself—have to say about his riches? "Behold, all was vanity

This week's reflections are written by Jessica Pisano, who is a member of Christ Fellowship Cherrydale in Greenville, South Carolina.

and a striving after wind, and there was nothing to be gained under the sun" (Ecc. 2:11). Really, Solomon? *Nothing* to be gained?

READ LUKE 12:13-34.

What does this passage say about possessions?

_____

_____

_____

_____

_____

It's interesting that Jesus connects the themes of possessions with envy, just like Solomon does in Ecc. 4:4. A man wants part of his brother's inheritance; Jesus' response is, "Take care, and be on your guard against all covetousness, for one's life does not consist in the abundance of his possessions" (Lk. 12:15).

What are some ways you are tempted
to envy the people around you?

_____

_____

_____

_____

Now, there are many reasons this fictional man might be so concerned with storing his possessions. It could be that he wants to impress those around him. It could be a sense of security he gets from his many possessions. It could be he just wants to relax and enjoy his life. A need for approval, a need for security, or a need for comfort are all very human, very relatable reasons to seek out money and possessions. Which of these reasons do you resonate with the most?

Jesus says, "You fool!" The rich man, like most of us, lets his need to impress, need for security, or need for comfort outweigh his soul's need. In doing this, he (and we) forgets two things:

First, we forget that in the end, his *soul* is required of him – he can't take these possessions with him. Solomon calls this a grievous evil: "Just as he came, so shall he go; and what gain is there to him who toils after the wind?" (Ecc. 5:16). Our existence is way bigger than this life we're in. If the vast majority of our existence depends on the state of our souls, then it would be foolishness to neglect it in favor of our fading and temporary possessions.

Second, we forget that we have a loving Father who provides everything we need. In the passage immediately following this, Jesus speaks gentle words of provision, comparing his people to the sparrows God feeds and the lilies he clothes. And "of how much more value are you than the birds!" (Lk. 12:24)

For our need to impress, He has given us Christ's reputation and standing before Him. We do not need to earn the approval of God or of people. In the most important way, we are approved of, accepted, celebrated, and welcomed. If we allow our identity as a beloved child of God to define us, there is no need to impress. No need to puff ourselves up. No need to measure up to those around us —we measure up to Christ.

For our need for security and reliable provision, He promises to feed us better than sparrows, clothe us better than lilies, and supply our every need. He made us with limitations, and He meets us in our limitations. We seek His kingdom, and He seeks our good.

For our need for comfort, He gives us His Spirit, His people, and a future treasure that will never get old or fail to satisfy. There may or may not be comfort and luxury in this life, but if we tend to our souls, we are guaranteed a perfect future with no more tears or sin or death.

Which of these promises are you prone to forget?

_____

_____

_____

_____

_____

_____

_____

_____

_____

_____

_____

_____

DAY SEVENTEEN

SCRIPTURE READING
1 Peter 1:3-9

Have you ever seen the videos of "The Candy Challenge" for toddlers? Parents put candy in front of toddlers and leave, telling the kid they will be right back. They say that if the toddler doesn't eat any candy, they'll get even more candy when the parents get back. We watch and laugh as the toddlers weigh their options, wondering when the parents will be back, thinking they might be able to get away with eating a little piece and still get more later. The toddlers have something good in front of them, but are challenged to hold out for something better.

We saw yesterday that to seek out wealth while neglecting our souls is foolish. Today we consider that seeking out wealth also isn't nearly as satisfying as we think. Sin always looks, sounds, or feels sweet, but ultimately leads to consequences, whether in this life or the next. Even things that are not intrinsically sinful always leave us wanting more. Shoes wear out, favorite clothes stop fitting, kids ignore toys, the thrill of the new wears off until we need another new thing. Solomon acknowledges this when he says, "He who loves money will not be satisfied with money, nor he who loves wealth with his income; this also is vanity. When goods increase, they increase who eat them, and what advantage has their owner but to see them with his eyes?" (Ecc. 5:10-11). The reality is that there are many good things in this world and in this life, but there is a much better thing to hold out for. We are all the toddlers in this scenario, but with much higher stakes.

The good news is that if we are in Christ, we have a treasure that is far greater than anything we could experience in this life.

READ 1 PETER 1:3-9.

What does this say about our inheritance in Christ?

_____

_____

_____

_____

Notice what is *precious* or *valuable* in this passage. One of them we don't have yet, but we look forward to it – our imperishable, eternal inheritance, which is being kept for us. It is waiting for us. It is impossible for it to disappear, be taken away, or be destroyed. Take that in – what a gracious God, who not only saves our souls from our sin, but actually rewards us for trusting in Him!

It's important to notice how we got to this inheritance – it's according to *His* great mercy, because *He caused* us to be born again. He has done the work and earned this inheritance for us, *and* we are currently being guarded by *God's power*. We did nothing to earn this reward, we are doing nothing to keep it, and there is nothing we can do to have it taken away. It is based on Christ's reputation, and not our own. It is in no way dependent on our actions.

Compare this inheritance with the wealth and possessions we tend to strive for in this life. We earn a worldly inheritance by our performance in our work, by our investing strategies, or our finagling of Facebook Marketplace, among other things. Our lives are full of hard work and striving. A wrong move can lose it all. Our earthly kingdoms are fragile. People spend their whole lives chasing comfort, security, and applause through money only to have it run out in this life or count for nothing in the next.

While details about our heavenly inheritance are few, we know it will be glorious and make every bit of suffering on this earth *worth it*. Any lack, need, or suffering we experience in this life pales in comparison with the glory awaiting us (Rom. 8:18; 2 Cor. 4:17-18). We know we will be in perfect harmony with God, that there will be no more tears, poverty, hunger, or unmet need. We will no longer be burdened by insecurity, self-absorption, or pride; we will be healed, whole, aware that we are loved. And if you need a description of the material heavenly city we will dwell in, read Revelation, where John hardly has words for it! Ultimately, this inheritance is one of *perfect belonging*. And this inheritance of belonging in this perfect place in a perfect relationship with God is indestructible. It is fixed and already existing. We can count on it. What an amazing thing to look forward to!

The other precious thing in this passage is one we *do* have now: our faith. It says our faith is more precious than refined gold. God is using our faith to powerfully guard us for our upcoming salvation. God's power through our faith is what gets us to our eternal and indestructible inheritance. We practice delayed gratification by training our time, energy, attention, and resources on our *faith*.

So, child of God, co-heir with Christ, ask the Holy Spirit. Are you living in light of your eternal, unearned, indestructible inheritance? What energy or resources are you spending on earthly treasures that could be redirected toward caring for your faith? Use the space to journal and ask God for help in this area.

_____

_____

_____

_____

_____

_____

_____

_____

_____

_____

_____

_____

DAY EIGHTEEN

SCRIPTURE READING
Mark 10:17-31

If you had a friend who knew you were making a bad decision but didn't warn you about it, would you consider them a good friend? If you shared that you're planning on eating spaghetti on a first date, a good friend might remind you of the slurpy, red-sauce-flying nature of this meal and suggest you steer clear. When you are pursuing something unwise people who care will tell you. This is proof of their care!

So, now that we see the surpassing worth of our heavenly inheritance, it seems only right that God warns us many times in his word about the danger of lesser, but tempting, pursuits, which are, of course, much more consequential than spaghetti.

READ MARK 10:17-31.

What does it say about people with wealth?

_____

_____

_____

_____

It would be easy to see this as a rebuke to other people, the "really rich." But we are all the rich young ruler. We are the "good person" with many possessions. We have more wealth and possessions than the majority of the world. And many of us know how to follow rules and how to be a "good Christian." We have a lot in common with this man.

So how does Jesus respond to the rich, to you and me? First, He looked at the man. He looks at us, makes eye contact with us. He _loved_ the man. His gaze toward us is full of love, understanding, and compassion for us. And out of that love, He told the man to sell his possessions and give to the poor so he would have treasure in heaven. He calls us to surrender, to trust Him, to have faith that He is better. He warns us in the following verses that wealth distracts us because it hardens our hearts to the surpassing worth and sufficiency of Jesus Himself.

This rich young man walked away sorrowfully and grieving, because he had many possessions. While he seemed to have surrendered his actions, he had not surrendered his wealth.

Now, God is not necessarily requiring you to sell all your things to give to the poor, but imagine He was. What reaction does that bring up in you? Are you willing? Joyful? Fearful? Uncomfortable? What does this tell you about your heart posture towards your possessions, and towards God?

Jesus' point here is that He wants full surrender. He says the rich man lacks one thing – this man had surrendered other parts of his life, but couldn't surrender this one. Is there part of your life you struggle to surrender?

These are difficult questions to think about! As you hear from the Spirit about this, remember that there is *great* comfort for us.

First, remember that Jesus says this out of deep love and care, knowing that there is a way *better* possession to be had. Like the friend warning you of danger, Jesus is warning us as well. To let go of the need to be financially comfortable makes complete sense if you believe the words of Jesus and really think that He is telling us this because He knows what we need.

Jesus' second great comfort comes after he shares that it is extremely difficult for a rich person to enter the kingdom of heaven. In the context of this story, it seems He is saying that those who have possessions have good reason to check their allegiance. The disciples despair, "Who then can be saved?" And Jesus responds, "With man it is impossible, but not with God; with God all things are possible" (Mk. 10:27).

What a reassuring reality for our fickle hearts! As we are lured away by shiny things, Jesus reminds us that it was never our power that saved us anyways. Our salvation has always been dependent on the mercy of God. When our grip tightens on our riches, and it feels so impossible to let go, Jesus promises that even this is not impossible for God. He can change your heart. Changing your heart is not just up to you—ask the Holy Spirit for His help!

Third, Jesus promises eternal life and a hundred-fold restoration of what we've lost for His sake. When we let go of earthly treasure for the sake of the gospel, we are choosing the better option. Would you take a thousand dollars now, or several million in ten years? When we zoom out and have an eternal perspective, it makes complete sense to set our sights on what is coming later. What we give up now for His sake will be restored with interest because He is generous.

Which of these comforts is most meaningful to you? Why?

_____

_____

_____

_____

_____

_____

_____

_____

_____

_____

_____

_____

_____

_____

DAY NINETEEN

SCRIPTURE READING

Acts 4:32-5:11

READ ACTS 4:32-37.

What was the early church's posture towards their possessions?

_____

_____

_____

_____

The Bible describes the early church as being "of one heart and soul" (Act. 4:32), and their unity immediately plays out in what they do with their stuff. Their attitude toward their possessions was, "it's not mine." They held their devotion to their things under their devotion to God and his people. And the effect on the community is that there was *not a need among them.*

I've seen this play out in my own life in a few ways: my parents are missionaries in Prague, Czechia. They have never owned a home; almost everything they have is borrowed and shared. Whenever they are away, their apartment is often used by someone who's in town. When we would visit the US growing up, everything we did depended on the generosity of someone else. A family vacation on the beach was possible because some believer owns a beach house and loves to bless missionaries. I got my car because a believer buys and sells cars affordably, specifically for people in ministry.

But this concept doesn't just exist in the missionary world; it plays out in our local church. When I was in college, I needed a place to stay and a family of five in our church opened their guest room to me for two summers. I got some tough financial news about student loans and our dear friends gave generously to meet that need. These are not especially wealthy people; they just see their houses, possessions, and money as not belonging to them. Friends, this is happening in our church! Is there a way God is asking you to be part of it right now?

Read Acts 5:1-11. Why do you think Ananias and Saphira lied and kept some money for themselves?

_____

_____

_____

_____

We all have a desire to be a part of something bigger than ourselves. As a teacher, I see students who are very difficult in one class behave totally differently in another, based on the culture of the group they are in. What culture is doing has a way of shaping what we think about and spend our resources on. God uses the church in a similar way, for good; the early church had a beautiful culture of giving so everyone's needs were met. What an amazing, God-honoring cultural movement! But God doesn't need us or our stuff – He wants our hearts. Ananias and Saphira gave, but their deceit reveals a deep commitment not to the things of God, but to their own reputation in front of other people. And their reputation didn't save their lives or their souls.

We've been reminded all week of one trap: the love of money. But here we see opportunities for sin even in our giving. When we give away our wealth, our motive can easily be to make much of ourselves. It is so easy to imitate Ananias and Sapphira in this way! Wanting to be god to another person or meeting a need so people will think highly of us totally misses God's heart in giving.

There is also a temptation to base our salvation on our poverty. This doesn't seem to be Ananias and Sapphira's motive, but it is worth mentioning here. I've heard this called the "Poverty Gospel," the idea that less we have, the more God loves us. The truth is that we do not earn God's favor by our poverty or the good work of giving wealth away. God's favor is lavished on us because of the sufficiency of Christ's sacrifice, not our wealth or poverty.

So we've been reminded all week that to cling to our possessions is sin, and reminded from this passage that even in our generosity there is opportunity for sin. Sin is everywhere we turn! "Wretched man that I am! Who will deliver me from this body of death? Thanks be to God through Jesus Christ our Lord!" (Rom. 7:24-25).

Thanks be to God, indeed! The reality in Christ is that there is *freedom* with our possessions. We are free to have them, because they are gifts God uses to provide for our needs and bless others. We are free to give them away, because it is not really ours and it is not our greatest treasure. But it is only when possessions are in their proper place, in submission to Christ, that there is freedom.

Which of these freedoms is most encouraging to you right now? How is the Holy Spirit challenging you in this area?

_____

_____

_____

_____

_____

_____

DAY TWENTY

SCRIPTURE READING
Galatians 6:7-10

We all have choices to make. There are many things outside of our control, but there are also many things God has given us authority over, especially in our western culture. We control how we spend our time, energy, attention and resources; we control what job we have and how hard we work; we control how we eat, how much we sleep, and what we put into our minds. It was one of the scariest things for me about moving out into adulthood — if I want change in my life, I'm the one that has to make it. It's exciting, and it's scary. There's no excuses, and I am not a victim of my circumstances. And all my choices have consequences.

READ GALATIANS 6:7-10.

What stands out to you from this passage?

_____

_____

_____

_____

Galatians is all about the choice we have between flesh and the Spirit, works of the law and faith, and the law and the promise. Near the end of his letter, Paul warns them: "Do not be deceived: God is not mocked" (v. 7). The world and the evil one try to convince us that this life is all there is, and that what matters is your current happiness and comfort. If you could chase after the things of this world and never experience consequences, God would surely be mocked. But he goes on to explain that we reap what we sow—chasing after the things of this world will absolutely bring consequences.

The farming language helps simplify this concept: if I plant (sow) seeds for tomatoes, I'll get (reap) tomatoes. If I plant onions, I get onions. I'm a terrible gardener, so there's no guarantee my tomato plant would produce tomatoes... but it definitely wouldn't produce onions. As surely as a tomato seed will produce tomatoes (not onions), sowing to the flesh will produce corruption.

Think about what you spend the most time, energy, attention, and resources on. In what ways are you tempted to "sow to the flesh"?

What does it mean that we will reap corruption? It reminds me of Matthew 6. First, it makes me think of Jesus' pleading to not store up treasures on earth, where thieves break in and steal, and moth and rust destroy. Stuff gets old, relationships are hard, people leave or let you down. Corruption. Secondly, it reminds me of the Sermon on the Mount, when He tells his disciples to fast, pray, and give in secret; those who do it in public have received their reward. In other words, if you invest in acquiring wealth and popularity in this life, that is all you'll ever get. You'll die and none of it will matter. Corruption.

The beauty here is that there's another side to it: if you sow to the Spirit, you will reap eternal life! As surely as an onion seed produces onions, investment in things of the Spirit produces a reward that far outweighs any earthly reward *and* lasts forever!

What does it mean to sow to the Spirit? The very next verse connects "sowing to the Spirit" to "doing good." The message of Galatians is that it's not your actions that save you, but faith. You don't have to fit a mold. Your salvation is in Christ, not yourself. In Christ there is glorious freedom, but don't use your freedom for evil. It's the Spirit that saved you, so continue walking in the Spirit and producing the fruit of the Spirit. Hang in there doing good – the reward is coming.

We can apply this to our attitude towards our possessions, too. It's not your wealth or your poverty that saves you, but faith. In Christ we have freedom with our possessions, but don't use this freedom to make much of yourself. Store up treasure in heaven, and use your possessions in this life to do good and honor God. Your greater reward is coming!

So we have choices, every day, and they have consequences. There's many things we don't have control over, but God has given us authority to choose the world or Christ. Don't be deceived – God is not mocked. Choosing the world means corruption, and choosing Christ means eternal life. Will we choose the things of this world, or the things of the Spirit? Will you store up treasures here or in heaven?

Christian, "do not grow weary in doing good, for in due time we will reap, if we do not give up" (Gal. 6:10). Your reward is coming!

How is the Holy Spirit encouraging
you or convicting you today?

_____

_____

_____

_____

_____

_____

_____

_____

_____

_____

_____

_____

_____

_____

WEEK
05

Work

ECCLESIASTES
2:18-26; 8:1-17

"I HATED ALL MY WORK THAT I LABORED AT UNDER THE SUN BECAUSE I MUST LEAVE IT TO THE ONE WHO COMES AFTER ME. AND WHO KNOWS WHETHER HE WILL BE WISE OR A FOOL? YET HE WILL TAKE OVER ALL MY WORK THAT I LABORED AT SKILLFULLY UNDER THE SUN. THIS TOO IS FUTILE. SO I BEGAN TO GIVE MYSELF OVER TO DESPAIR CONCERNING ALL MY WORK THAT I HAD LABORED AT UNDER THE SUN."

ECCLESIASTES 2:18-20

"THE PLACE GOD CALLS YOU TO IS THE PLACE WHERE YOUR DEEP GLADNESS AND THE WORLD'S DEEP HUNGER MEET."

FREDERICK BUECHNER,
WISHFUL THINKING:
A THEOLOGICAL ABC

DAY TWENTY-ONE

SCRIPTURE READING
Genesis 1:1-25

When you spend any amount of time in his writing you can't un-see it—King Solomon has a tendency, throughout his poetic book, to paint the idea of work in a very unpleasant light.[6] We see this as a common thread throughout his writings in the book of Ecclesiastes: everything is meaningless; vanity; of no importance —especially our work.

In Ecclesiastes 1:3 he says, *"what does a person gain for all his efforts that he labors at under the sun?"* In other words, at the end of our life, what is there to show for our whole life being committed to a work that brings toil and labor?

Later on in Ecclesiastes 2:17 he states, *"therefore I hated life because the work done under the sun was distressing to me. For everything is futile and a pursuit of the wind."* And a few verses

[6] This week's reflections are written by Allysa Trainer, a member of Christ Fellowship Cherrydale in Greenville, South Carolina.

later he says: *"For what does a person get with all his work and efforts that he labors at under the sun? For all his days are filled with grief, and his occupation is sorrowful; even at night, his mind does not rest, this too is futile."*

As a result of the fall of man and the entrance of sin into the world, our work is now cursed, void, and just plain hard. Read Genesis 3 if you need to refresh your memory! There are thorns and thistles everywhere, and we experience the sweat of futility as we labor in this infested Garden.

This is really, really unfortunate news for those who work—which is all of us in some capacity. If all of the claims that King Solomon makes about our work are, in fact, true, this leaves us with little to no hope for the work we spend so much time laboring in, whether that be working a 9-5 job, raising children and caring for a family, or getting an education in preparation for a career in the future.

But there is hope, and it's found in the way God created work in the first place. In Genesis 1, we see God model meaningful work.

READ GENESIS 1:1-25.

What does Genesis 1 show us about God? What does it have to do with how we think about work?

_____

_____

_____

_____

_____

In Genesis 1, we see the triune God actively at work. God is bringing the universe into existence through His spoken word, and His Spirit is hovering over the waters. This story of creation gives us a foretaste of what we see God doing all throughout the redemptive story of human history: God works.

Not only do we see God the Father at work in Genesis 1, we also see God the Son and God the Spirit working as well. All three are active participants in creation. In John 4:34, the Son (Jesus) says, *"My food is to do the will of Him who sent me and to finish His work."* The work that the Son was doing was bringing redemption to the world.

In John 14:26 we see Jesus telling His disciples about the promise of the Holy Spirit their Counselor. The Spirit works to call to mind the words and teachings of Jesus. We also see how the Holy Spirit actively works as the one who guides in truth. John 16:13 says, *"But when he, the Spirit of truth, comes, he will guide you into all the truth. He will not speak on his own; he will speak only what he hears, and he will tell you what is yet to come."* The Holy Spirit has come to us (just as He came to them!) so that we can intimately know Him, follow His voice, and remain faithful to the work He's given us.

So we see all persons of this triune God at work. And when we take a look back into the text of Genesis 1, we see that everything He made was good, and everything He made brought life. This is how God works and how we are to work—We strive to do **good** and give **life** through meaningful labor.

Genesis 1 is a model for the type of work that God wants from people who reflect His image. People continue the work of God in the world, which infuses the laborious nature of fallen work with purpose, even if that purpose is somehow limited. We work to do good and give life and now we do this with the Spirit's help.

Not only did God work, but He also continues to work. If you stop to think about it, each of your days is filled with countless examples of God's work. Sadly, we don't often stop to take notice of the ways that God is at work around us. So as we begin this week, jot down a few examples of ways that you see God at work in your life and in your world.

_____

_____

_____

_____

_____

_____

_____

_____

_____

_____

_____

_____

_____

_____

_____

_____

DAY TWENTY-TWO

SCRIPTURE READING
Genesis 1:26-31

The first thing we learn about God in His Word is of His eternal existence, one that has no beginning nor end. We know that He is triune, three in one. And before He is a creator, He is a Father, constantly delighting in and extending His triune love. And it is out of this triune love that God creates. And create He did. He exercised his creativity, power, and life-giving love through the creation of the world, breathing all of life into existence.

We see him speaking life into the night sky and daylight; the water and land; the creatures of the sea and the creatures on the dry ground. They were created and deemed "good." However, in Genesis 1:26-27, we see a change in how He describes His creation. God says, "Let us make man in our image, according to our like-ness. They will rule the fish of the sea, the birds of the sky, the livestock, the whole earth, and the creatures that crawl on the earth. So God created man in His own image. He created him in the image of God; he created them male and female.

When God breathes life into the creation of mankind, He breathes His image into them. This can't be missed! Mankind—of you and I—uniquely carry the image of the triune God. All creation prior to this moment points towards the creativity of God, demonstrating His loving care, but now we see a distinct difference between the creation of mankind and the creation of everything else: man and woman are created to *reflect* God Himself.

We not only are crafted by the Creator with precision, thoughtfulness and immense detail, but we *bear the marks of His image*. What immediately stirs up inside of you (thoughts or feelings) when you dwell on the truth that you are a new creation and are uniquely made to carry the image of God Himself?

_____

_____

_____

We reflect part of His nature and character to the rest of creation. It is equally a great gift and a great responsibility to bear His image in all that we do. We bear this image in our relationships, our rest, our play, and even our work. As His anointed image bearers, we are now sent out into the world to do His will & work, in all things bringing the Kingdom of God to earth.

We are called, as His image bearers, show compassion and care, provide for the poor, seek justice for the voiceless, and to "preach the

Gospel to **every** creature" (Mk.16:15), and to bring freedom, peace, and reconciliation of God to all people, by His name and in the anointing and power poured out on us by the Spirit.

As we unconditionally love, faithfully serve, fervently pray, and boldly proclaim the truth of Jesus' resurrection to a lost and dying world, we are fulfilling the joyful duty of bearing His image. We do not work from a place of obligation, but because we've been invited to participate and delight in the Trinity. To work with the same Jesus that taught us to pray "Your Kingdom come, Your will be done, on earth as it is in heaven" (Matt. 6:10).

God joyfully invites us to step into this work alongside Him. We feel pressed by the Spirit to share the gospel so we do. We flee from evil and pursue what is good. We work to heal broken relationships. We steward creation. We strive for justice and exercise mercy. There is much good to be done! This is what we choose to walk in when we step into a relationship with, and follow, Jesus.

It is a "whole of life" path that encompasses and transforms every aspect of our lives. It drastically changes how we engage in our homes and neighborhoods; our relationships; our environments and our everyday sleeping, eating, going to work, walking-around life (Rom. 12:1). We can be certain that this call to meaningful work extends to our workplaces as well.

This "whole of life" invitation is for all. When God says "that the whole world would know and worship Him," He wasn't extending the invite to a select few that labor crossculturally. It's for all who call Him our Father.

The invitation is for those who labor down the street, in the classroom, in a hospital room, and at the kitchen sink. Any and all roles we play, or work we find ourselves in, are ordained out-workings of the role we play in following Him. The vocations we hold are simply the way we flesh out the work He has laid before us, and it's the way we express our love for Him and to Him, putting into practice our service for Him.

Ultimately, if we want to partake in bringing His work and will to fruition; and we say yes to this beautiful and open invitation to work alongside our heavenly Father in bringing redemptive restoration; in joining Him in making all things new - it has to begin and end with Jesus, with what God has already been doing since the beginning of time to bring new life. We work in co-mission WITH Him in His transforming activity to earth. Our efforts at the edge and His work front and center.

This is what we have the joy in laboring for.

Think about the places you find yourself laboring. Try to identify where and how you have seen God already at work. What evidence can you look for that God is working?

_____

_____

_____

How can you join Him this week in the work He is doing?

_____

_____

_____

DAY TWENTY-THREE

SCRIPTURE READING
Genesis 3:8-19

It was in the middle of the night and I was awoken (yet again) by the cries of my newborn twins. I was tired. So, so tired. And overwhelmed. Frustrated. Anxious. You name it. But nonetheless I pulled my half-awaken body out of bed and walked into the nursery. I remember sitting on the floor of the twins bedroom, feeding them for the millionth time, working so hard to get them burped, in clean diapers, and back to sleep, all without them waking the other one up.

And all for me to fall back asleep and do it again an hour later.

Amidst two screaming newborns that couldn't be soothed, I cried out in frustration, "God, this is too hard for me. I'm not cut out for this! I'm tired! I feel alone! The incessant cries are pushing me over the edge. WHY is this so hard and where are You right now?"

The work that has been given to me was (and still is) hard and there are no shortcuts around it. I am limited, my best efforts still aren't enough, and left on my own I cannot tend to it faithfully.

READ GENESIS 3:8-19,
what are some things we learn about work after the Fall?

_____

_____

_____

When Adam and Eve sinned against the Father, God did not make them work as a form of punishment. Rather, the work they were already doing was now cursed. Work, in its original form, was designed to bring life, joy and renewal. But now, because of sin, work is marked by toil, curse and death. The beauty of work was tainted. The Fall makes work exhausting, and the significance of rest established in creation is buried under our physical need for rest. In a world that is broken, people rest as a means to an end.

As we live as sojourners in this world we know the hard won't go away until we are united again with Christ—our work will forever bear some mark of sin—but that doesn't mean He leaves us to work without hope. Because of Jesus, our work can be redemptive and purposeful.

Instead of believing that God was reigning above, placing us into hard spaces of work as a form of some cruel punishment, what if we chose to flip the narrative and believe that God placed us in the hard for a holy purpose? What would change in our work if we knew that

God, in His depths of wisdom, did not just ordain the hard, but was with us in it?

In His kindness, God places work in front of us as a gift that is for our good and for His glory. Redeeming our once "cursed work" to a holy restoration.

Ultimately, God is more concerned with what He's doing in us rather than the work we're doing for Him. Colossians 3:17 states, "*And whatever you do, in word or in deed, do everything in the name of the Lord Jesus, giving thanks to God the Father through him.*" It's because of this that the most mundane task of our day can be transformed into something glorious in His sight.

For the believer it's about our "long obedience in the same direction." Because of Jesus' resurrection from the dead, we can have hope that He is at work - even when the work is hard and life is frustrating.

He gives us an invitation to engage with our work in a new way. Instead of asking questions like "why me?" or "why now?", we can walk confidently alongside our Father, asking Him to give us eyes to see how He sees and how He is wanting to work in us through the hard circumstances of life. His priority is for Christ to be formed in us (Gal. 4:9) and that can almost always guarantee sharing in Christ's sufferings.

Work is hard and the ground is cursed, but God is the God of resurrection who specializes in making peace from chaos and bringing dead things to life. We can then truly believe that no matter what we see or can't see, God is able to redeem our efforts for our good and His glory.

Yes, work is hard. It will always be hard. But the hardness of our work gives us the unique opportunity to anticipate the day where the ground will no longer be cursed and Jesus will make all things new. and in the meantime we can rely even more deeply on the work of His grace to sustain us.

The work that has been given to us is hard and there are no short-cuts around it. But God can do more than we ask or think, His presence is enough, and He will never leave us because He's promised to love us to the end.

Take a few moments and list out some of the hard things that God has given you in this season, as you list them, remember that God's ultimate concern is that He is formed in you. Ask Him how He is wanting to form you more into His image through the hard things He has ordained.

DAY TWENTY-FOUR

SCRIPTURE READING

Exodus 31:12-17

In our culture and society, we exalt productivity. Work is a sign of our strength and rest is our weakness. We wear our long work hours, our busy schedules, and even our burnout as a badge of honor. The daily grind is what gives us value and significance. And oftentimes, when we rest, we are led into uncomfortable spaces and are forced to confront who we are apart from our striving.

Rest on the seventh day of creation, is the very first time we see something be "hallowed" in God's Word. This day of rest is set apart, like God is set apart in His holiness. The Father diligently labors in his work of Creation for six days and says it is all "very good." And then He ceased from His work.

What feelings bubble up inside of you when you think about resting?

_____

_____

_____

In Genesis 2 God both works and rests. From His example, we know that God does not undervalue work or think it to be unimportant. God created us in His image and with a specific job in mind: to be responsible over creation. So the fact that He creates us in His image and entrusts us with very important work proves that He intends for us to be about the business of faithful work. On the other hand, it is also clear that God does not need rest because of physical tiredness or fatigue. And He also does not need to rest to regain energy to produce more work, since we see Him modeling rest at the end of creation.

For us to work without rest or rest without work is to live outside the framework God established. There is something more to our rest that God is wanting to invite us into. What is it that God wants us to experience through our submission to rest?

In the Old Testament we have some more understanding surrounding the purpose of rest.

READ EXODUS 31:12-17.

What do you observe about this passage?

_____

_____

_____

There are two things we can learn about rest through this passage from the Old Testament. First, our keeping of the sabbath is a way for us to live out this special communion with God as his children. The sabbath has been given as a sign, pointing to the covenant between Israel and God. This sign of rest is not passive, but rather active, it is real participation with God in the delight of resting in his creation.

Second, we see the sabbath functioning as a day when God Himself is refreshed, and he desires for us, as his children, to experience that same refreshment! Our rest from our work—our sabbath—invites us into a sacred space of being in intimate communion with our Father and experiencing the refreshment he wants us to give us. Hebrews 4:9-11 says, *"therefore, a Sabbath rest remains for God's people. For the person who has entered His rest has rested from His own works, just as God did from His. Let us then make every effort to enter that rest, so that no one will fall into the same pattern of disobedience."*

The Israelites had failed to take up God on his invitation to enter into rest with him, resulting from their disobedience to him. But there is good news for us as followers of Jesus! Because of Jesus' sacrifice, we possess the opportunity to accept this invitation of rest, regardless of who we are or where we come from. We rest in Jesus, not necessarily on a singular day.

What a gift and honor to be invited into this sacred space. Sabbath is holy because it is a day that belongs to our Father, but praise be to God he doesn't hold it closed handed but rather he graciously chooses to invite us into it. And not only does He invite us into it, He relishes in us and communes with us when we are there with Him.

May we step into that invitation today, yielding ourselves to the vast generosity of the provision that he meets us with in it—Himself. May we let go of the work we foolishly claim as our own and leave it at the feet of Jesus. Knowing that his finished work for us on the cross gives us the freedom to accept our limitations, do our work faithfully with a posture of dependency on his perfectly finished work, and rest with him in the grace he lavishes on us in spite of ourselves.

Ask the Spirit to reveal to you what is hindering you from entering into rest with Jesus. Where are you looking for rest outside of Jesus? Are there thoughts or circumstances that are all consuming? Are there desires/idols that you are clinging to, in hopes they will provide rest? Habits that need to be reevaluated that leaves no space for rest?

_____

_____

_____

_____

_____

Ask Jesus that He would enable you to die to the false sense of self-sufficiency and embrace his perfect rest. How is the Spirit leading you to practice entering into the rest he wants to give you today?

_____

_____

_____

_____

DAY TWENTY-FIVE

SCRIPTURE READING
2 Corinthians 5:16-21

The Japanese have an art form, *Kintsugi*, that involves repairing broken pottery by mending the areas of breakage using lacquer mixed with gold. *Kintsugi* is birthed from the idea that by embracing flaws, you can create an even stronger, more beautiful piece of art. The breakage is part of its beauty. Every crack is unique and instead of repairing an item, the technique actually highlights the "scars" as a part of its unique design. There is no attempt to hide the damage; the repair is highlighted.

When I professed faith in Jesus, I received not only a Savior of my sins but also a Redeemer who is actively working to restore every second, every aspect of the broken places of my life—including the broken spaces of my work. Just as Jesus' scars highlighted his victory over death, so would He allow my scars to function not as a defect, but a proclamation of His glory. And it's through His healed wounds that Jesus' scars forever proclaim our final victory in Him.

But it's easy for all of us to forget that right? I know this to be true for my own life. When bedtimes aren't going the way I hoped they would go. When the laundry has piled up and I can't keep up with any of it. When three tiny humans are demanding every part of me emotionally, mentally, and physically. I forget. I forget in those moments that God is redeeming. That he is inviting me to experience redemption and freedom by participating in bringing His kingdom to earth through the broken places of my work. So often, I operate my life (and my work) out of the reality of Jesus' death but not of his resurrection.

READ 2 CORINTHIANS 5:16-21.
When you think about your own life, are there any areas
where it's hard to remember the new creation that you are
in Jesus and your redemption in Him?

_____

_____

_____

Because of His finished work on the cross we have been delivered and redeemed from the strongholds of sin and no longer live as a slave to our flesh. Rather, we are a new creation who has been fashioned to serve our creator in the way that we work. 1 Corinthians 10:31 tells us that whatever we are tasked to do, we now do it in light of being a new creation and living in the hope of his resurrection. Because His Kingdom operates on a completely different set of values, now even the mundane task has meaning. We are working as a redeemed people, living in God's kingdom here on earth.

But it is still in this space where we live in tension. We are experiencing the "already coming" kingdom of God, and yet we are still sojourning through the "not quite yet" fulfillment of all things. Because this kingdom has not fully come, we are still passing through, still longing, still working in broken spaces as broken people.

Tish Harrison Warren describes this tension in a beautiful way, stating that we hold two realities hand in hand. Our work co-labors alongside God's work in bringing light to darkness. But our work doesn't cease to exist in real darkness. It is still a place of futility, where we are constantly rubbing up against the brokenness of the world we live in. We live in this toiling state (Ecc. 2:17-26). We sow but we hardly reap. We fail. The word of God consistently differentiates between the good work we have been created to fulfill and also the real, active residence of drudgery in it. Our work really is a place of toiling, pain and hardship because of the thorns and thistles, both literal and metaphorical, that surround us. But that is not the end of our story.

So we must ask ourselves, how does our redemption in Jesus through His death and resurrection affect our work? Why not just keep our face to the ground and hold our breath till His return?

In the passage from 1 Corinthians 5, we learn that God has given us both a message and a ministry focused on reconciliation. God has entrusted us, as His people, to use the broken work spaces we find ourselves in to bring about this reconciliation. And our message and ministry is not arbitrary. It's right here and now—happening in real time in the world we're living in.

In the same way that Kintsugi artists repair pottery, God uses our lives, our work, to accomplish His purposes of repairing brokenness in the world. He has given us a message and ministry of reconciliation and He's making his appeal through us. One beautifully broken piece at a time.

So with what He's given us in mind— think about how this reality translates into your life. Where are the areas you have been given to work? Who are the people God has given you? Are there places near you where you know there's a need for renewal?

_____

_____

_____

_____

_____

_____

_____

_____

_____

_____

_____

_____

_____

WEEK
06

Wisdom

ECCLESIASTES
3:1-15

"HE HAS MADE EVERYTHING
APPROPRIATE IN ITS TIME.
HE HAS ALSO PUT ETERNITY IN
THEIR HEARTS, BUT NO ONE CAN
DISCOVER THE WORK GOD HAS
DONE FROM BEGINNING TO END."

ECCLESIASTES 1:8

"Beauty doesn't take away the pain of
suffering or vulnerability. It's not like cicada
song or good coffee make it hurt any less to
lose a spouse or a friendship, or even just to
have a hard day. But in the times when we
think anguish and dimness are all there is
in the world, that nothing is lovely or solid,
beauty is a reminder that there is more to our
stories than sin, pain, and death. There is eternal brilliance. It's not quite enough to resolve
our questions or tie anything up in a nice
metaphysical bow, but sometimes it is
enough to get us through the next hour.
And in enduring a mystery, we need just
enough light to take one more step."

TISH HARRISON WARREN, *PRAYER IN THE NIGHT:
FOR THOSE WHO WORK OR WATCH OR WEEP*

DAY TWENTY-SIX

SCRIPTURE READING
Genesis 8:15-22

Our foster daughter was sunshine—not the kind you find in the sweltering, blistering heat of summer, but the very start of fall sunshine.[7] It was the kind of sunshine that is cool and warm at the same time, and that beckons you to bask in the oncoming autumn. Our girl was as smart as a whip and hilarious; she noticed everything, and she had this charm about her that drew people in. As bright as her light shone, there were inevitable clouds that came. If you looked closely enough, you could see the storm coming that

[7] This week's reflections are written by Laura Campbell, a member of Christ Fellowship Cherrydale in Greenville, South Carolina.

threatened to smother her fire that had carried her through so much darkness in her life. Often, we would be blindsided by it: the hurricane of trauma responses and huge emotions that ripped through our home and our souls. The task of loving her, of being a consistent and compassionate presence for her, felt huge. And honestly, it felt like too much to bear, and I questioned why God invited a couple of newly married twenty-somethings like us to take on this girl and everything that came with the world of foster care. We knew that saying yes to this invitation meant that everything would change, we just had no idea that it would change us to our very core.

One thing that we can always count on in this life is that everything changes. Often, the changes we encounter feel like a breath of fresh air, like those few weeks between summer and winter when the trees that cover the Blue Ridge Parkway burst into a symphony of gold, orange, and red. Or the day that you finally get to pull the first box of Christmas decorations out of storage. However, everyone is deeply acquainted with changes that, instead of sparking excited anticipation, mark moments of entering into seasons of doubt, mourning, or weariness.

Solomon really doesn't make the reality of shifting seasons in life seem all that appealing. Times to mourn, die, tear down, weep, and uproot? Solomon asks a profound question in light of all of this: *"what do workers gain from their toil?"* (Ecc. 3:9).

Nobody gets to escape the reality of the broken world that we live in. For every moment of good that fills our hearts, we can also recount seasons of life that bring ache. So what do we do when we come face to face with seasons that we desperately want to turn and run from?

Here's a place where I think Noah might offer some help.

_____

_____

_____

Obediently, Noah built the ark, anticipating the coming rain. As the sun shone down without a cloud in the sky, God finally told him to get on the boat; suddenly, *"all the sources of the vast watery depths burst open, the floodgates of the sky were opened, and the rain fell on the earth forty days and forty nights."* (Gen. 8:11-12)

And then Noah waited.

As the rain relentlessly beat down upon the earth, and the floodwaters washed death over everything that was living, Noah waited on the Lord. And we have to wonder: in the 10+ months that Noah was sitting on that boat, did he ever think to himself, "Hey God, do you remember me down here? I'm still just floating!" Did he ever question if he heard the word of the Lord correctly by the time he reached month five, six, seven of waiting? That is our human nature, isn't it? As we sit in a dark season of life, we are prone to wonder if God remembers us at all. It's easy to wonder if the sufferings we endure will ever cease, and it's hard to remember that we do not wait without purpose and hope.

When we reflect on Noah's story, we see a God that doesn't break His promises. He remembered Noah, his family, and every single animal. We see a God that wipes away evil and establishes a covenant with His people that death will never have the final say.

God tells Noah, *"As long as the earth endures, seedtime and harvest, cold and heat, summer and winter, and day and night will not cease"*

(Gen. 8:22). In the darkest night, we know that daytime is coming. Every tiny seed placed in the ground will bloom. Because we are citizens of the kingdom of Heaven, there is hope as we wade through every season on this side of eternity. We know the ending of the greatest story that has ever been told—an ending marked by victory over sin and death. An ending that is marked by a promise fulfilled. An ending that is really a new beginning. Every moment that feels like we are floating on a boat in the middle of deep water with no hope of land in sight, He is growing the longing in our hearts for eternity.

What are we tempted to believe about God in seasons of darkness?

_____

_____

_____

_____

What is the truth about God that we
can hold onto when faced with shifting seasons?

_____

_____

_____

_____

_____

_____

DAY TWENTY-SEVEN

SCRIPTURE READING
Matthew 13:24-30

The nature of suffering we don't like to acknowledge is that, on this side of eternity, bad and good coexist. When it seems like God is providing everything we could want or need, it's easy to believe that is how His goodness shines in our world. We think He's clearly active when He provides healing in sickness, community for the lonely, a child for the barren. It's easy to conceptualize this "vending machine god", but in an upside down Kingdom where the last is first, the persecuted are blessed, and the Messiah of the world is born in a lowly stable, we learn that it is not on the mountaintops where we are assured of His faithfulness. Rather, our most broken and needy places are where we know God greater.

MATTHEW 13:24-30.

What stands out to you in this passage?

_____

_____

_____

A man planted his crop, and when he wasn't looking, an enemy came to sabotage his efforts by planting weeds to overtake the good seeds. This idea is familiar to many followers of Jesus: our plans and seeds we have sown play out exactly as we hope until suddenly, we get hit by a curveball. The loss of a family member, getting laid off from work, tension in friendships, mental health struggles... When dreaming of the future, nobody thinks to add "*in a few weeks, I will start preparing for an adverse life event today that I think is coming tomorrow*" to the family calendar.

But things always happen, don't they? Things are completely out of our control, and we don't have any choice except to keep moving forward despite each obstacle we encounter. The farmer in this parable knew immediately what had happened—an enemy had come, weeds were entangling the wheat, and he had no option except to let it grow together, lest he also uproot the wheat. In this parable, God is not following a step behind the farmer to pluck out every weed before it can bring any harm to the crop. Rather, He compels the farmer to allow the bad to take root right next to the good, and wait as they grow together. This is how the Kingdom comes.

We learn very quickly as followers of Jesus that the way of Jesus is not a smoothly paved and linear path. As humans, we want the path of least resistance: the path with signs that clearly point which direction we are to walk and when we are to walk them. We want the parenting book with a step by step manual for every possible situation and children who are born able to follow along with the script. We want to throw seeds of the Gospel in the hearts of unbelieving people and be able to see the roots take hold in their hearts right then and there. Often, we want to believe that the way of Jesus does not require seasons of sitting in hurt and suffering. We much prefer vending machine Jesus that gives us a roadmap that points out clearly what we should do next. It is hard to acknowledge the lived experience of most followers of Jesus: that He is asking us to walk down that path that He knows will lead us through seasons of pain.

Reflect on a season in your life where Jesus was asking you to walk through hurt and suffering.

The man who planted the seeds in this passage makes a significant statement: the enemy is the one who planted weeds to strangle the good that was growing. And not only that, he knew that he could not rip the weeds out of the crop without bringing harm to the growth of the wheat. It was probably incredibly tedious and frustrating for the man to go back through his field and meticulously unravel weeds from the wheat once everything was fully grown and ready for harvesting. We can imagine the sun beating down on him and the ache of crouching in the field all day to preserve the good growth against the bad.

When we walk through seasons of hardship and growing pains, it can feel like evil is right on our heels and attempting to squash the fruit that has bloomed during our journey. But like the farmer that did not rip out the weeds when he saw them growing in his crop, our posture is not that of someone running scared from what suffering might do to us; rather, we square our gaze on the cross, we acknowledge that the pain and hurt are very real and present, and we harvest the fruit that blooms in the midst of suffering.

What truths have you learned about Jesus in the midst of walking through seasons of waiting while suffering?

_____

_____

_____

_____

How do these truths affect how you interact with and love fellow believers and nonbelievers?

_____

_____

_____

_____

_____

DAY TWENTY-EIGHT

SCRIPTURE READING
2 Corinthians 5:1-10

Our culture is obsessed with staying young and beautiful forever. The commercials are everywhere: buy this to get rid of the wrinkles around your eyes from smiling too hard. Get this to hide the dark spots on your face. Without these little fixes for our changing bodies, someone might dare to guess your age, and even worse, they might guess correctly! Our bodies carry evidence that we are finite people living in bodies that won't stand the test of time. We will age, and our bodies will inevitably show it. But it makes sense, right? The things that are made for earth cannot last for eternity. We are waiting for something better than this.

READ 2 CORINTHIANS 5:1-10.
What do you observe about Paul's idea of a tent?

_____

_____

_____

Paul likens our earthly body to a tent. A tent is flimsy, never completely protected from the harsh elements of nature, and not very comfortable if you plan to be there for a while. And no matter how long you plan to camp in that tent, its purpose is still to be a temporary shelter. This body that we live in is not the final destination for us. This is great news for us, because as Paul points out, our bodies are constant reminders that we are not where or how we are meant to be. As we age, we wrinkle and ache. Our minds are heavy with the weight of our experiences, and our bodies show the evidence. From birth to death, our bodies are in a constant state of aging and evolving, and we are reminded that we are not meant to be here forever.

Luckily the story does not end there: as followers of Jesus, we know that there is hope as we see the decay of our earthly bodies. Paul reminds the church, "we have a building from God, an eternal dwelling in the heavens, not made with hands" (2 Cor. 5:1). We have more than this life to set our sights on; we have a heavenly dwelling waiting for us. And not only is this heavenly dwelling waiting for us, but we are also eagerly awaiting our new body.

It is not easy to keep our sights set on things eternal while we wait in a body and world that will not last. On earth, our bodies and souls are afflicted with illnesses, injuries, heartbreaks, losses, and so much more. As we walk through each season of life, our bodies wither, and it can seem like our souls wither under the heaviness of sin. But we have a promise: "He who has prepared us for this very thing is God, who has given us the Spirit as a guarantee" (2 Cor. 5:5). Some translations say that we have the Holy Spirit as a "down payment."

This is our hope: the Holy Spirit dwells inside us, and while our bodies waste and wear under life's burdens and afflictions, the Spirit remains unchanging and ever present with us as we wait for eternity with the Father. Even though we are only in a temporary body right now, we have a foretaste of intimacy and nearness because of the Spirit dwelling inside of us. Because of this, we can do more than put our head down and simply survive the afflictions on this side of heaven; rather, the Spirit spurs us onward to be of good courage through all of it. As Paul reminds us in 2 Corinthians 5:9, our aim is to please our Maker through the power of the Holy Spirit, not just to merely exist in this body. Let this truth be your song of hope: that we are made for so much more than just enduring all of the pain we are experiencing.

In light of this, Paul tells the church how we can live confidently because the Spirit of God dwells with us, inside of us, always: we walk by faith, not by sight (2 Cor. 5:7). Walking by faith is not possible without the Spirit. Through every trial in life that makes us feel like we are being beaten down, the Spirit that dwells within us is a constant reminder that there is so much more than what we can see and feel right now. Our home, our future hope, is awaiting our arrival. The Spirit, the "down payment" (2 Cor. 5:5) for our future home in eternity, is constantly urging us to lift our eyes up to the heavens and continue in confidence that we will one day put on our heavenly dwelling and say goodbye to this flimsy tent of a body.

The hope of heaven, our eternal home, is assured for the believer. We don't have to wonder about the purpose or the futility of life under the sun, because we know the end of this story. In Ecclesiastes, Solomon reminds us that God has "put eternity in their hearts" (Ecc. 3:11). We are spurred onward because of the seeds of hope God planted on our hearts. Through every season of life, our confidence is that home is coming.

**What causes you to forget to walk
in hope and faith?**

_____

_____

_____

_____

_____

**How does 2 Corinthians 5:1-10 bring you
hope in your current season of life?**

_____

_____

_____

_____

_____

_____

DAY TWENTY-NINE

SCRIPTURE READING
Isaiah 40:27-31

The two best moments of a race are the very beginning and the very end. Right before a race starts, as the runners are shoulder to shoulder at the starting line, hearts are pounding with adrenaline as they wait for the whistle sound. Cheers erupt from the onlookers as the whistle kicks things off, and runners' eyes are filled with determination as they put into practice all the techniques that are meant to sustain them to the finish line. The real test, however, is found in the middle of the race after the adrenaline wears off, and there's nobody to cheer and spur you onward. It becomes a mental battle just as much as a physical one: knowing that there is still so much farther to go, and you still have to muster the strength and mental determination for a little while longer to get to that finish line.

The life of the follower of Jesus can feel like a marathon, and Solomon begs the question: "what does a worker gain from their toil?" (Ecc. 3:9). For the Christian, the gain is not found in being the fastest runner on the team that wins first place every time. The prize is really found in the struggle and the moments when you don't know if you can go on, and every step is accompanied with crying out, "Jesus, restore and renew me again." For the believer, all seasons of life, whether good or bad, are not simply followed by renewal of the Spirit. Rather, renewal is intimately intertwined through every step along the way.

READ ISAIAH 40:27-31.

What do you notice about God's posture to one who is weary and worn out? How does God respond?

_____

_____

_____

The moment we surrendered our souls to the Lord and became followers of Jesus, we entered ourselves into a race, and we don't reach the end until we meet our Creator face to face. The race to eternity does not measure our success by our strength and grit, or about how you place or what your record time was. In the upside down kingdom, it is not the strongest and fastest athletes that receive this renewal. Instead, our aim is to constantly turn our face to the One who is able to restore the breath in our lungs. We see that "youths may faint and become weary, and young men stumble and fall, but those who trust in the Lord shall renew their strength" (Isa. 40:30-31). It is those who are weak and wanting, those who are desperately needy of restoration, that receive the renewing power of God. The Gospel that saved us from death will also renew our bodies, our souls, and our faith on a day by day, moment by moment basis.

As a runner breathes deeply and intentionally through each step, so should the follower of Jesus call upon the name of the Lord every moment. It is our lifeline, our oxygen to get us to the finish line where we will be with God. Because of this promise for restoration, we know that God is not simply waiting on us at the end of the race, but rather, He is with us every moment of the race, constantly empowering us to continue running.

READ ISAIAH 40:28-29.

Why can we have confidence that the Lord will renew us daily?

_____

_____

_____

He is our source of life as we race to eternity. Solomon reminds us, "everything God does will last forever" (Ecc. 3:14). We can confidently call upon the name of the Lord for renewal in any season, knowing that what He says and does is not only good, but it is lasting, and His faithfulness to do as He says He is going to do is not contingent upon our own strength.

If you've never seen a toddler try to do distance running, it goes something like this: they take off in a sprint with arms flailing at their sides, and either they stop seconds later, breathlessly turning to mom and dad to be carried, or they trip over their own feet and faceplant. Often, this is also followed by a comment from mom that sounds something like, "I knew that was going to happen." And still nothing could stand in the way of a parent that is running to pick up and comfort their child after they have fallen. Just as parents can predict their child falling before it happens, our weariness and need for constant renewal is no surprise to God. Renewing us is not His obligation. It is His delight.

How can you practice asking Him for renewal this week?

DAY THIRTY

SCRIPTURE READING

Ephesians 3:14-21

Through one of the darkest seasons of my life, I felt this tugging at my heart, a request from God asking me to submit to what He has in store for me. That season of life lasted throughout the entire year of 2020, which also happened to be the worst year ever for the whole world due to the COVID-19 pandemic. It felt like there was no end in sight— that the grief and bitterness festering in me would grow so big that it might swallow me whole.

My mind did not have the strength to sit in the Word, as it left me with more brooding questions than answers, and my faith that was hanging on by a thread only found solace in listening to worship music. I found myself on my knees, emotionally, often literally, asking God, *what on earth do You want from me?* And eventually the questions grew to sound more like, *God, do You even care?* It's a question that I had never pondered long enough to unpack until that time in my life. Through the everchanging seasons of life, what is it that God wants from us?

READ EPHESIANS 3:14-21.

What do you notice here?

_____

_____

_____

_____

Paul wrote to the church in Ephesus when he was imprisoned, and for a guy who was a prisoner, he doesn't sound all that worried. Not only does he call himself a "prisoner of Christ Jesus" (Eph. 3:1) and "an ambassador in chains" (Eph. 6:20), but he also refers to his imprisonment as "the stewardship of God's grace that was given to me" (Eph. 3:2). Paul considered his imprisonment as his divine appointment in God's plan, a grace of God. Now don't get me wrong– I don't think Paul was happy about his lot. We can imagine this time might've been filled with fear and wondering what God's next move was going to be. But despite the fear of his current position in God's plan, Paul shows us in Ephesians 3 two ways to position ourselves in light of God's movements in our lives:

→ **We submit ourselves to His way**

→ **We root and ground ourselves in His love**

141

Paul writes to the Ephesians that he "bow[s] his knee before the father" (3:14). Throughout the story of the Bible, those who fought against the will of God did not have things go well for them (we're looking at you, Jonah). There is no doubt that you have had moments in your life where God was asking you to submit to His plan, and you fought against Him. Friends, there is grace in this. What we see in Ephesians tells us that we can trust that God's way is good. Solomon also reminds us that "He has made everything beautiful in its time. Also He has put eternity on man's heart, yet so that he cannot find out what God has done from beginning to the end" (Ecc. 3:11). He is able to do far more abundantly than we ask or think, so we can trust that even if His ways make no sense to us right now, that we can still submit ourselves to His plan. His plan for us is good, even if it doesn't feel good.

Paul is also inviting the church in Ephesus to lean more deeply into God's love for them, to be rooted and grounded in it. Our lived experience, not just our hope, is that we are loved by God with a love that, according to Paul, surpasses our knowledge. So we are not loved the way you love your spouse, parent, child, sibling, or friend, but His love for us is as incomprehensible to our finite minds as the distance of the farthest star in the sky. And if God can cradle the expanses of the universe in his hands and still watch over the sparrow, then how much greater is His love for you? Whatever season you are walking through, you are being held in love.

There is another important moment in this passage. When speaking of comprehending the greatness of God's love for His people, Paul tells the church, "...that you, being rooted and grounded in love, may have the strength to comprehend **with all the saints** what is the breadth and length and height and depth, and to know the love of Christ which surpasses knowledge..." (Eph. 3:17-19). We don't have to figure all of this out on our own. As believers, we can expect that whatever season of life we are in, we will be in it *with* other believers who are being the hands and feet of Jesus. We can know that the act of *being with* is not a burdensome task, but a holy one. To stand beside a brother or sister in times of joy, grief, celebration, waiting, or all of these things at one time, is a task of stepping into the way of Jesus. Joining hands in this way is receiving a small, earthly glimpse of more to come— something incomprehensibly greater than anything we've ever known.

We can confidently bow the knee to the will and way of God, because all wrongs will be made right, and everything will radiate His glory. In every season of life, God is asking us to submit His plans and His ways and to live loved by Him.

Where in your life is God asking you to submit to His way?

_____

_____

_____

_____

_____

_____

_____

_____

_____

WEEK 07

Death

ECCLESIASTES
3:16-4:3

"FOR THE FATE OF THE CHILDREN
OF ADAM AND THE FATE OF
ANIMALS IS THE SAME. AS ONE
DIES, SO DIES THE OTHER; THEY
ALL HAVE THE SAME BREATH.
PEOPLE HAVE NO ADVANTAGE
OVER ANIMALS SINCE
EVERYTHING IS FUTILE."

ECCLESIASTES 3:19

"I walked a mile with pleasure;
She chatted all the way;
But left me none the wiser
For all she had to say.

I walked a mile with sorrow;
And ne'er a word said she;
But, oh! The things I learned from her,
When sorrow walked with me."

ROBERT BROWNING HAMILTON

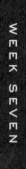

DAY THIRTY-ONE

SCRIPTURE READING
Isaiah 53:1-6

Death and I became acquainted with each other in May 2020 when I sat in an ultrasound room, waiting to hear what would happen to our unborn baby.[8] I had been to funerals before, but never anything like this. As I lay there, watching on the screen as our little girl's heart was beating and she sucked her thumb in utero, we were told to get ready for the worst. Trying to grasp any shred of goodness I could find, I asked the doctor if there was any hope that she would live, and I was met with a tentative and saddened, *"there is typically no hope in these situations."* As the following days unfolded, she was right about one thing and wrong about another.

This is what she got right: we would lose our girl in the following days. Those days were shrouded in grief and sadness that slowly turned into anger and bitterness. Cries of "Your will be

---

[8] This week's devotions are written by Laura Campbell, a member of Christ Fellowship Cherrydale in Greenville, South Carolina.

done" morphed into "You were supposed to prove everyone wrong and let her live, because that's what God does—the impossible." I only wanted to believe in a God that let everyone live—a God who molded His will and way to fit into my definition of what goodness and happy endings should look like. Anything else felt utterly unfair.

In Ecclesiastes, Solomon speaks of life under the sun as full of wickedness and injustice, and pondered if the life and death of people was any different than that of animals. He claims, "everything is futile" (Ecc. 3:19), and that it's better to not even exist at all. Maybe our modern equivalent of Solomon's ponderings is, "what's the point of it all?" I imagine that a lot of people who have lived any length of time on earth have wondered this. What is the point of all this living and dying when the life that we find in between is laced with so much heartache? Often, instead of looking upwards, we turn inward and ask, where is God when the world's economy of justice feels nothing short of brutal and unfair?

READ ISAIAH 53:1-6.

What do you observe about what Jesus' life on earth was like?

_____

_____

_____

_____

Isaiah describes the life of Jesus as one that was full of sorrow and grief. He wasn't liked by many people, he wasn't the most handsome guy to look at, and He was afflicted with grief and sorrow. We see in Isaiah 53:5, "but he was pierced for our transgressions, he was crushed for our iniquities: upon him was the chastisement that brought us peace, and with his wounds we are healed." In this verse is a man that bore everything on our behalf: *our* transgressions, *our* iniquities, *our* chastisement and wounds. Every horrible thing that was meant for us, He carried. Why would one man—the only perfect person on earth—take onto Himself the weight of the world's injustices? To what end?

This is the greatest injustice: that the faultless Lamb was to die in the place of sinners. And yet, despite the unjust nature of it all, He willingly turned His face to the cross, blood and sweat upon His brow, and took our place in the name of love. Isaiah states, "All we like sheep have gone astray; we have turned–everyone–to his own way; and the Lord has laid on Him the iniquity of us all" (Isa. 53:6). Jesus, who bore death so we did not have to, is intimately acquainted with our grief. Through the torture He endured, He didn't have to ask the Father "what is the point of all this pain?", because He knew the greater purpose of it all and that life was waiting just around the corner. Death can feel like a lonely place, but we know that there is One who has gone before us. Our hope is found in the unshakable truth that death does not have the final say for the follower of Jesus.

This is what my doctor got wrong that day: believing there was no hope. As humans, our hope is often misdirected. We believe hope means that the story always ends wrapped up in a pretty bow and a happily ever after—that God should fix us before we have a chance to break instead of believing that He can bind up all of our broken pieces. Friends, this is where our hope lies: "with *His* wounds, *we* are healed" (Isa. 53:5). In our times of greatest affliction, we can experience hope knowing that the place we are in is a place that Jesus has been already. Our grief, sorrows, sadness, and losses are familiar to Him who bore the weight of the world as he hung on the cross, waiting for death to come but never being overcome by death. The story of the Gospel is the story of a man conquering death, rising again, and bringing restoration to His people.

Reflect on the moments in your life that feel marked by death or an ending: death of a family member or friend, death of a dream, or a friendship ending. Where do you see evidence of His faithfulness to you?

_____

_____

_____

_____

_____

_____

_____

_____

_____

_____

_____

_____

DAY THIRTY-TWO

SCRIPTURE READING
Isaiah 61:1-3

A characteristic of Jesus that we see regularly is that He is always on the side of those who are least loved by society. We see this throughout all of Scripture: the most surprising people, those with the lowest social standing and regard, are those who Jesus chose to surround Himself with and pour out His blessings on. He dined with tax collectors, and He told His followers to posture themselves like little children. When Goliath should've won by a landslide, David found victory against the giant in a small stone and the power of God behind him. This is who God is: the One who is for the weak and the poor in spirit.

READ ISAIAH 61:1-3.

What is the Lord's posture towards those who are
facing injustice and those who mourn?

_____

_____

_____

_____

This passage carries great hope to those who are walking through mourning as it describes what the Messiah will do when He comes. The hope we hold on to through injustice of all kinds is that our God hates the oppression of His people, and that His mission is to heal all those who are brokenhearted.

Brokenheartedness is not limited to physical death. Most people are eventually touched by the death of something in their lives: we are all familiar with the death of future dreams, the death of hope, the death of feeling safe and secure, the death of choices, the death of a relationship. Things fall apart, and as humans, we strive to grasp at the broken pieces in our lives and to hold it all together.

As we carry some of these heartbreaks, every person who has ever been a part of our story has carried their own stories of brokenness. It seems so unjust to us when our stories of brokenness and mourning don't get to have a pretty bow wrapping up the end of a happy story.

Now read Matthew 27:15-23.

What we see as injustice could be the vessel that God uses to unfold parts of His redemptive plan for His people. Barabbus was the criminal who was meant to pay for his crimes, but was chosen to walk free, and

Jesus was put in his place. Barabbas is described as a "notorious prison-er" (Matt. 27:16). When presented to the crowd, the priests and elders had already convinced the people to demand Jesus' execution instead of Barabbas'. So Jesus, the Healer, lover of those on the outskirts, the Son of God, went in the notorious criminal's stead to die. The crowd of people did not care about what was right and true, only that Jesus would suffer. And here's the good news: Jesus was not surprised at this chapter of the greatest story ever told—that a criminal would walk free and that He would soon die on the cross as an innocent man.

So He went willingly, sorrowfully, accepting the cup before Him, yet still knowing that true justice is waiting at the end of this story. And it was not only Barabbus' crimes, his sins against God, that resulted in Jesus hanging on the cross; it was all of us. Our sin sat on the Spotless Lamb's shoulders; He remembered our names as He went to die, and He did so with love for us and obedience to God's redemptive plan.

But this is the heart of God– that the burden of our sins is not placed on our shoulders; rather, the Son drank the cup of God's wrath in our stead, making the greatest injustice the salvation of the world. God's eternal purposes cannot be thwarted by anything, not even an unjust and cruel death, because even death could not keep Jesus in the grave. The risen King is our eternal hope: our lifeline in the face of in-justice and death. When it feels like the heartbreaks and deaths that we carry are forgotten by God, remember that His plan, the unfolding story before us, is that all things will be made right. When hope feels hard to come by, we are assured in Isaiah that the ending of the story is beauty instead of ashes (Isa. 61:3).

What are the heartbreaks that you are carrying?

Write out a prayer to Jesus telling Him about your hurt, and ask Him to help you experience His comfort and hope.

_____

_____

_____

_____

_____

_____

_____

_____

_____

_____

_____

_____

_____

_____

_____

_____

_____

_____

DAY THIRTY-THREE

SCRIPTURE READING
Psalm 6:1-10

One of the realities of death is that it takes more from us than just one moment of tragedy and loss. Death requires our conscious engagement on a continual basis. We remember the pain of loss physically through sleepless nights, leaving our bodies feeling worn down. Our minds become clouded with overwhelming sadness, maybe even depression and anxiety. When death claims someone in our lives, the aftermath feels like a plague inside of us—body and soul. But that is the nature of grief, and we as Christians are often uncomfortable approaching this inevitable part of our faith walk. It's overwhelming and exhausting to relive moments of deep anguish that stain our lives. Grief pops the bubble of innocence that we once lived in and forces us to acknowledge that things are not right in this world.

In my own experience with the death of someone I loved, underneath all of my sadness and anger was confusion. The process of losing our unborn daughter felt like a hurricane that swept through a sunny day. In the wake of her death, I didn't know how to reconcile the parts of the Bible that promised that God was truly near with the ache inside of me that was icing over my heart and making me cold to God's promises and the truth of the Gospel. I felt like I was sitting in grief with nowhere to go but down, deeper into my sorrow. I wanted God's promise that He would be near to me to mean that I didn't have to hurt anymore—that I could get a vision of His divine plan of redemption to allow death in this life to make more sense.

I asked God, with anger and accusation in my heart, what He could possibly be doing to make any of this right again, and what He compassionately met me with was something I never knew to ask for. There was an invitation to experience something more in the midst of the anguish: an invitation to lament.

READ PSALM 6:1-10.

How would you describe David's tone in this chapter?

_____

_____

_____

_____

We see expressions of lament all over the Bible. This particular passage ends with acknowledging that the Lord heard his plea, but many of them don't. Many of David's poems and songs of lament start and end with telling God that he feels lost in the darkness—this is the outpouring of grief. The sadness, anger, confusion, numbness, or anxiety that follows death is the experience of grief, but lamentation is the expression of grief.

In the Psalms, David repeatedly cries out to the Lord, and not all of those moments are neat and tidy. Often his questions for the Lord feel full of accusation and anger at God. They are riddled with "why?" and "how long?"

Instead of internalizing our grief and allowing it to fester in our hearts, lamenting is the avenue for the Christ follower to invite the Father into our experience. And the exciting part of this is that however we lament, maybe through quiet, tearful prayers on our commute to work or through shouting and shaking our fist at the sky, God is big enough to take whatever it is we have for Him. No matter our questions or crying out, God is readily listening with a compassionate invitation to draw closer to Him.

Here is the beauty in the messiness of lamenting our sorrows to the Father: lament actually has the power to change us from the inside out. It won't erase the pain, but it brings something more to the table. Lament requires us to consider the fact that in our crying out to the Father, in reaching our hand in broken desperation, He just might actually be there. Grief and suffering, when wielded by the enemy, often fool the Christ follower into believing that He is far away from us, not listening compassionately, and willfully turning His face from us in our time of need. However, when we choose to lament our losses and our hurts in light of God's faithfulness and Jesus' work, we are posturing ourselves in a way that invites the only One who has the power to heal into our grief.

READ PSALM 6:8-10.

What do David's words about the Lord's posture to him do inside you?

_____

_____

_____

_____

_____

_____

What are your losses/sorrows/deaths that the Father is inviting you to lament?

_____

_____

_____

_____

_____

_____

DAY THIRTY-FOUR

SCRIPTURE READING
Job 30:16-20

Everything happens for a reason.
God needed another angel in heaven.
God will never give you more than you can handle.
God works everything for good.

You've heard all of this before. Maybe you've even said this to people before (I know I have!). When people we love are going through loss, it makes sense that we want to make it better. We like to pick our way through the Bible in order to find pockets of hope when we are walking with someone grieving. We love the moments of "I will fear no evil" (Ps. 23:4), but not so much the moments of "my only friend is darkness" (Ps. 88:18). Now, I don't think that next time you are walking alongside someone who is grieving that you should whip out a coffee cup with, "God is testing them that they may see that they themselves are but beasts" (Ecc. 3:18) in all caps as a healthy dose of reality, but I am saying that, in our efforts to encourage brothers and sisters with Christian clichés, we might be doing them a disservice. What would it look like in the Church if, instead of accidentally pushing each other to run away from the pain, we encouraged each other to grab ahold of the pain and grief with both hands as we run towards the throne of God.

"Look at the bright side" Christianity is lacking an incredibly important layer of relationship with God. When we only allow ourselves to follow-up our pain and suffering with "but God working all this out for His good," we are robbing ourselves of a level of intimacy with God that invites us to offer our anguish to Him. We are simply floating on the surface when there is so much more in the deep end. This is when lament enters the picture: our crying out, our questions, and our exclamations to God. So when we are confronted with death, how does the Christian lament?

READ JOB 30:16-20.

What do you notice about Job's lament to God?

_____

_____

_____

_____

_____

Job was brutally honest with God. Throughout his story, he does not cover up his sadness or try to pretend that he doesn't fear what is to come. Job asks God some really hard questions, and gives God the unedited, unabridged experience that is going through his mind. He tells God that he feels alone. He tells God that it feels like he has been overcome with affliction. Later in the chapter, Job says that God has become cruel to him. Can you imagine accusing God of being cruel? God must have punished Job for that one. Except... He doesn't. God does not get frustrated at Job's human nature that wants answers. God doesn't get offended at his accusatory tone and lack of eternal foresight. In response to Job's expression of grief, *his lament*, God reminds Job of who He is and what He has done.

So what does it look like to lament? We see it throughout the whole Bible:

- Jesus asks the Father while on the cross, "Why have you forsaken me?" (Mat 27:46).

- Job expresses that he wishes he had never been born (Job 10:19).

- Davids expresses, "I am weary with my crying out, my throat is parched. My eyes grow dim waiting for my God" (Psalm 69:3).

- Mary tells Jesus, "Therefore, when Mary came where Jesus was, she saw Him, and fell at His feet, saying to Him, "Lord, if You had been here, my brother would not have died." When Jesus therefore saw her weeping, and the Jews who came with her also weeping, He was deeply moved in spirit and was troubled" (John 11:33).

All of these moments are expressions of deep grief that resulted from death and loss. They are questions, exclamations, the deepest longings of their hearts. Our offerings of lament are a way for us to reach out our hand to God whose hand is always readily open for us. When we dare to speak out loud the questions we have for God, we receive God's invitation for an honest and intimate relationship with Him. Lament is openly expressing our pain and fears. Lament is asking hard questions, even if we might not get an answer. Lament is the raw, honest truth of the state of our hearts. This is where we meet Jesus in the wake of death: not with a big, shiny bow that beautifully wraps up our grief with happiness, but in accepting His gentle invitation to lament.

How can you practice lamenting this week?

_____

_____

_____

_____

_____

What are questions or thoughts about your experiences with
death that you have been afraid to speak out loud to God?

_____

_____

_____

_____

_____

_____

DAY THIRTY-FIVE

SCRIPTURE READING
Psalm 30:1-12

I used to imagine grief and joy sitting at a table together, and on my hardest days, I imagined the two arm wrestling. Whoever won got to take up the most space in my heart and mind. Through the process of lamenting, of turning my mourning into an offering, what once felt like an arm wrestling match turned into grief and joy shaking hands, both in agreement that this space is now to be shared. This is the tension we embrace as followers of Jesus: that grief and joy share a home in our hearts—both necessary and belonging. So what does this mean for the believer? When we are confronted with this tension of grief and joy stirring inside of us, one thing we can know is that Jesus is inviting us into something.

The invitation is not a fast-track ticket out of discomfort. The discomfort we will experience from this tension will be an ongoing, maybe daily battle, but Jesus has the power to use our experiences with death to transform our worship of Him and how we understand His posture towards us.

READ PSALM 30:1-12.

How do you see the Lord respond to David?

_____

_____

_____

_____

When you are intentionally inviting Jesus into your grieving, worshiping through loss and lament can bring you into deeper, more intimate worship with the Father. Even if your lament feels full of anger and hurt, you are still turning your attention to God and bringing those frustrations as an offering at the feet of the only One who has power to do anything about it. Our hearts are still drawn closer to Him when we pour ourselves out in this manner. This is an act of worship. When we embody the posture of giving ourselves to God in whatever state we are in, we are worshiping Him by embracing the fact that we have belonging with Him even as our most broken self. For the believer, this means that God does not expect us to show up polished and buttoned-up; even when you feel like you have nothing to give, the broken pieces of yourself will be transformed into something new. In Psalm 30, we see the psalmist sing praises to the Lord in worship, and in the very next sentence, cry out and plead to the Lord for mercy—this pleading and crying out is also an act of worship. Through David's act of pleading, God brought renewal to his mourning, and turned it into dancing. In our despair and suffering, we are still broken worshippers. This is where we find restoration.

When we make space for broken worship, it softens us to the body of worshippers around us. For the believer that has walked through death and loss already, you are able to stand in solidarity with the newly suffering person. You have the awareness and experience to be able to invite your brother and sister to stand next to you on the solid ground you have found in your own process of lament. Grief and lament give us a new lens to see others walking through suffering and walk with them more meaningfully, but we don't have to have shared experiences of loss to be able to stand in solidarity with the Church. Often, we get stuck on feeling like we don't have the perfect words or help to bring to someone in a season of suffering, but despite your lack of experience with losing a friend, parent, sibling, or child, our hearts still break for our friends who are suffering. Lean into that heartbreak on behalf of your brother or sister: this is where lament can be lifted up on their behalf. There is so much more power in standing with a grieving friend and praying aloud, "God we are hurting and confused and don't know where You are in all of this," than scrambling for the best quick-fix answer. The power of the body of believers linking arms together in suffering is found in this space of shared grief.

So what can we do in the wake of loss, whether it be our own or a brother or sister? We worship and embrace the transformation that is taking place in our hearts, softening us to the world we live in, and walk beside other broken people as fellow broken people. This is our invitation.

If we allow ourselves to see what is possible in the aftermath of death, we just might find that the biggest change in us is that we can see God's posture towards us more clearly. The Father does not watch us lament our losses with a cold heart and from a distance. He draws near, and His Spirit grieves along with us. He is a compassionate and faithful companion to us. Our God is a "with" God, a compassionate listener, a loving Father, and faithful Friend– not a bystander watching from a distance as we wade through the currents of grief. No matter what it is that you are walking through, He is *with* you.

What do you think God's posture towards you is when you are going through grief and suffering?

Write a prayer of lament, for yourself or for a friend you know that is suffering.

WEEK
08

Obedience

ECCLESIASTES
5:1-7

"GUARD YOUR STEPS WHEN
YOU GO TO THE HOUSE OF GOD.
BETTER TO APPROACH IN
OBEDIENCE THAN TO OFFER THE
SACRIFICE AS FOOLS DO, FOR THEY
IGNORANTLY DO WRONG."

ECCLESIASTES 5:1

"We live in what one writer has called the "age
of sensation."" We think that if we don't feel
something there can be no authenticity in
doing it. But the wisdom of God says something
different: that we can act ourselves into a new way
of feeling much quicker than we can feel ourselves
into a new way of acting. Worship is an act that
developsfeelings for God, not a feeling for God that
is expressed in an act of worship. When we obey
the command to praise God in worship, our deep,
essential need to be in relationship with God
is nurtured."

EUGENE H. PETERSON, A LONG
OBEDIENCE IN THE SAME DIRECTION:
DISCIPLESHIP IN AN INSTANT SOCIETY

DAY THIRTY-SIX

SCRIPTURE READING
1 John 5:1-4

All couples exchange vows at their wedding.[9] Sometimes they might write their own vows, other times they use a set of vows that have become standard: They go something like this:

I _____ , take you _____ , to be my husband/wife, to have and to hold from this day forward, for better, for worse, for richer, for poorer, in sickness and in health, to love and to cherish until we are parted by death.

These are not merely cute statements to fill time in a ceremony. They are intended to give voice to promises that each spouse is making to the other. That's what a vow is—a person giving his or her word, in the presence of dozens or even hundreds of witnesses, about what he or she intends to do.

[9] This week's reflections are written by Matt Rogers, one of the pastors of Christ Fellowship Cherrydale in Greenville, South Carolina.

Vows wouldn't have the same impact if they said something like:

> As long as I feel like it and you treat me well, I might continue in this marriage. However, should someone or something better come along or should you fail to live up to being the spouse that I think you might be, then I will leave you and find someone else.

Vows are statements of fact. They are promises. They aren't hypothetical. Solomon, in Ecclesiastes 5:1-7, writes about vows people make to God. On the surface, it might sound odd to talk about vows to God, but my guess is you've made your fair share of them through the years. Maybe at the end of a convicting sermon you promised God that you would change something about your behavior. Maybe on a retreat you felt prompted to step up your game in some way and you told God you would do just that. Maybe you got busted in some sin and you promised God never to do it again. Or maybe you were walking through something really hard and you told God that you would be faithful if He would just let the outcome of the suffering play out as you wanted. We've all made these kinds of promises.

Solomon makes a simple point: If you tell God you are going to do something, you should do it (Ecc. 5:4).

READ JOB 30:16-20.

What do you notice about Job's lament to God?

_____

_____

_____

_____

Love.

Love is the basis of marriage vows. We do what we say in our vows because we genuinely love the other person, and we express that love through our faithfulness. Even if there were to come a time down the road when our loving feelings abate, we still keep the vows we made to our spouse because we know that we committed to love them.

God says that His children love Him. Love for God is a defining mark of a Christian. Something fundamentally changes when people are converted. Their affections change. They go from loving the world and sin to loving God and righteousness. Since God's children now have the love of God flowing from their new heart (Jer. 31:31-34; Ezek. 36:24-28), they express that love to God through their obedience to His commands.

In our day, many Christian leaders and pastors challenge the notion of works based salvation, or the idea that the forgiveness of my sins and my right standing before God is based on my holiness. It is good and right to explain that moralism isn't the gospel. The danger, however, is that we can easily fall into the other error. Throughout church history, this error would be referred to as "antinomianism." It's a big word that's best understood in two parts—"nomas" means "law" and "anti" means "against." So antinomians are "against the law." They believe that good works of obedience to the law aren't essential for Christians. Since good works don't save, they argue, good works don't matter.

John and Paul would passionately disagree. Hear how Paul argued this point in Romans 6: "What should we say then? Should we continue in sin so that grace may multiply? Absolutely not! How can we who died to sin still live in it?" (v. 1-2). God's children love God so they don't keep sinning. They strive to obey. Obedience matters.

174

MATTERS OF THE HEART

In what area of your life do you need to
show God you love Him by obeying Him?

_____

_____

_____

_____

_____

_____

_____

_____

_____

_____

_____

_____

_____

_____

_____

_____

_____

_____

_____

_____

WEEK EIGHT

DAY THIRTY-SEVEN

SCRIPTURE READING
Jonah 2

It's hard to imagine what you would do if you spent 3 days hanging out in the belly of a big fish. We have TV shows like *Alone* that feature men and women who are isolated in a deserted place and have to find a way to survive. But that's not even close to the reality Jonah experienced when he had to endure the dark, smelly, damp confines of the fish stomach. You'd imagine that if you were in such a predicament you might make a few promises to God along the way.

"God, if you will get me out of the fish alive then I promise I will do what you've asked me to do."

"I'll clean up my life. Follow your path. Worship you forever."

READ JONAH CHAPTER 2

and notice what Jonah does there.

Jonah calls out to God in his distress and begs God to save His life. If anyone does, Jonah surely knows that his salvation is dependent on the Lord. After all, you don't just find a way out of the belly of a fish. Someone has to get you out.

Have you ever been in a place like this? Of course, none of us have been trapped in the belly of a fish (at least, I don't think you have), but I bet we could all think of a time in our lives when we felt trapped. A good illustration of this is any type of addiction. When people are battling addictive behavior they often recount feeling trapped. They might want out of the deadly cycle, but they keep going back. Like Jonah, they feel engulfed, overcome, as if their lives are fading away. It's a terrible place to be.

But you don't have to be addicted to drugs or alcohol, for example, to feel trapped like this. People feel trapped for all sorts of other reasons too. It could be trapped in cycles of anxiety or depression that plunge you to the depths of despair. You might feel trapped with sins of lust or anger. You could feel trapped in a marriage that feels like it's unfixable.

These examples are some of the reasons why the Bible speaks of sin as slavery. Jesus is clear, "...everyone who commits sin is a slave of sin" (Jn. 8:34). To sin is to be trapped in sin, like Jonah was trapped in the belly of the fish.

When we are there, we tend to make promises to God akin to Jonah's vow. We aren't told exactly what the vow entails. Likely, it involved Jonah making a promise to do what God asked Him to do and heading to Nineveh to preach there (see Jonah 1). What we are told is that Jonah pledges to offer a sacrifice to God by fulfilling the vow he'd made (Jn. 2:9). He knows that salvation is the Lord's alone so he's dependent on God to get him out of this mess, and, if and when God does, Jonah will do what God has asked Him to do. Jonah will fulfill HIs vow.

Think back in your life to a time when you felt trapped. What did you tell God in those moments? Did you make any promises about what you would or would not do when you got out of your mess? Now fast-forward to the present version of yourself. Are you pursuing faithfulness in the areas you promised?

Take marriage for example. It's common to meet a college student who is trapped. Let's use a guy as an example. He has no prospect of dating on the horizon and he's trapped in cycles of pornographic addiction. He can't stop looking at porn and he sees no chance of ever finding a wife, much less a godly wife with whom he can raise a family and worship God. So he cries out to God, "Please help me! Make a way for me to have a wife to love and cherish. Give me purity of thought and mind to pursue her and her alone. If you do, God, I promise to make my marriage a thriving picture of your love for your people. I will honor and love her faithfully as long as I live."

Fast-forward to today. That same guy has been married to a godly wife for a decade now, and they have three kids. On the surface, he's got everything he asked for and more. But he's dissatisfied. He tends to notice nothing but his wife's faults. He rarely tells her she's beautiful and seems to have no desire for intimacy. He serves begrudgingly around the house and bemoans any expectations she might place on him.

It's a pitiful scene that gets replayed over and over again. We make and break promises to God left and right. Jonah and Solomon both remind us that this is not right. So too does James when he writes "so it is a sin to know the good and yet not do it" (James 4:17). If you know the good you should do and pledged to do that good in a vow to the Lord, then it's not legalistic to say that God expects you to do what you said.

Where do you need to keep a vow that you've made to God?

_____

_____

_____

_____

_____

_____

_____

_____

_____

_____

_____

WEEK EIGHT

DAY THIRTY-EIGHT

SCRIPTURE READING
Isaiah 1:10-15

"You are all talk!" You may have heard this jab from time to time. It's leveled against someone who talks a big game but doesn't tend to back it up.

READ ISAIAH 1:10-15.

What do you notice about God's accustation here?

_____

_____

_____

_____

God speaks through His prophet Isaiah, who brings a strong word of critique and challenge. The people bring offerings, they make sacrifices. They are active, but they aren't faithful. They were doing the things that God asked His people to do. Sacrifices aren't wrong, in fact, they were expected. So what was wrong?

The people were merely going through the motions of these outward actions, but their hearts were not in love with God. They were disobedient in the normal rhythms of life (i.e "your hands are covered in blood" v. 15) even as they continued to come to the temple, offer sacrifices, and engage in the various trappings of religion. Back in 1 Samuel 15, God told the Isrealites: "To obey is better than sacrifice" (v. 22). In other words, there was something behind the outward acts of sacrifice that God expected from the people. It wasn't merely bringing a bull or a goat and killing it on an altar. These were merely external actions that expressed the semblance of worship to God. They were acts of obedience, meant to flow from a heart of obedience. So if you take the heartfelt obedience out, then the sacrifices don't matter. You can't place a veneer of religious activity over an otherwise unchanged heart.

Today's Christians aren't offering animal sacrifices, but we are often guilty of the same sin that plagued Israel. It's easy to become infatuated with the outward markers of religious expression, but do so out of obligation or routine, not love.

The implications of this sin are stunning if you think about it. Notice Isaiah 1:15: "When you spread out your hands in prayer, I will refuse to look at you; even if you offer countless prayers, I will not listen." There are times when God says He will not listen to people's prayers, much less answer those prayers.

On this side of the death and resurrection of Jesus, the blood-guilt that was due for sin has been poured out on Christ. Christians are forgiven for sin—past, present, and future. God hears their prayers, not because of their moral perfection, but because of the imputed righteousness of Christ. All this is good news for sinners like you and me.

However, this good news should not obscure the fact that our ongoing sin matters. If it was true that God did not want mere outward acts of worship in the Old Testament, how much more would this be true for those who have been saved by Christ's work and given His Holy Spirit as a gift. We should watch our lives so that we avoid going through the spiritual motions. Similar to Isaiah, Jesus accused the religious leaders of His day:

> Woe to you, scribes and Pharisees, hypocrites! You clean the outside of the cup and dish, but inside they are full of greed and self-indulgence. Blind Pharisee! First clean the inside of the cup, so that the outside of it may also become clean. Woe to you, scribes and Pharisees, hypocrites! You are like whitewashed tombs, which appear beautiful on the outside, but inside are full of the bones of the dead and every kind of impurity. In the same way, on the outside you seem righteous to people, but inside you are full of hypocrisy and lawlessness (Matt. 23:25-28).

Outward conformity, but inner rottenness.

Outward sacrifice, but inner hypocrisy.

Jesus pronounces "woe" on people like this. It's a word that denotes a warning. Jesus is saying that if this is true for you, then you should assess your life and make the necessary changes.

Today many people, especially those who live in cultures where Christianity is the dominant religion, are tempted to keep up their spiritual practices even if their hearts aren't right with God. They go through the motions of Bible reading, prayer, church attendance, even church leadership, while coddling unrepentant sin in their hearts. The prophet Isaiah called these "useless offerings" (Isa. 1:13). In contrast, Paul called Christians to offer their whole lives to God as a living sacrifice, and he called these acts of worship—good and pleasing to God (Rom. 12:1-2).

What would be a good and pleasing act of worship for you today?

_____

_____

_____

_____

_____

_____

_____

_____

_____

DAY THIRTY-NINE

SCRIPTURE READING
Romans 5:12-21

Keeping our promises is hard work.

Remember the last diet or exercise plan you tried to execute? Or maybe the last New Year's Resolution you made? Many times, we know the good that we should do, but we still struggle to do what we tell ourselves we will do for more than a couple of weeks at a time. Then, maybe a year or two later, we come back to the same issue and have to try again to make progress.

The same pattern plays out in our spiritual lives. We often know that we should read the Bible or pray or share our faith, but we just can't seem to find any consistent rhythms with these disciplines. So we bounce back and forth between making promises to God and then feeling guilty when we don't keep those promises.

READ ROMANS 5:12-21.

Why does this passage say people give in to sin
and struggle to pursue righteousness?

_____

_____

_____

It might be nice if we were born morally neutral and simply had to make up our minds to do good. This is likely the way many envision the spiritual state of humanity. Not too good. Not too bad. Just right in the middle with the inherent power to determine if they want to go forward or backward.

But this is not how the Bible portrays us. Scripture consistently says that people are born dead in sin. In our passage today, Paul says that all sinned in Adam. In other words, when Adam sinned in the Garden all people sinned. His sin infested the entire human race so that all people are now born hostile to God and unable to do anything morally good. It's no wonder, then, that people can't keep their promises, whether they be promises that are made to God, promises made to others, or promises made to themselves. Sin has so infested the human condition that apart from the work of Christ and the power of the Holy Spirit, we can't please God.

And therein lies the hope. We do not have to stay "in Adam." We can be reborn "in Christ." Just as Adam's sin spread to all people, so also Christ's righteousness spreads to those God saves.

Have you ever thought about why the life of Jesus Christ matters? Many times when we talk about salvation, we focus on the death and resurrection of Jesus, and rightly so. But if all Jesus came to do was die in our place and rise again victorious over death, then He certainly could have died as a baby. But Jesus lived for over three decades on this earth. His life is more than simply a moral example for us to follow. Rather, he lived without sin for all these years. He built a portfolio of righteousness for all to see. This righteous life was what God wanted from all people, but they were unable to be perfect. Jesus did what they could not.

And He gives this righteous life to Christians as a gift. There's a theological term for this gift—many refer to it as "imputed righteousness." We know that righteousness means moral perfection. What does imputed mean?

You might be helped to contrast "imputed" with "earned." Earned righteousness is what we deserve through our moral effort. It's what happens when we think about people being born in a morally neutral state and working really hard to please God through their actions. If they do enough good works, then the moral scales tip in their favor and they've earned blessing, forgiveness, and eternal reward.

In contrast, the idea of imputed righteousness flies in the face of earning. Imputation means something that comes from the outside and is placed in us or given to us. Some even use the term "alien righteousness" to denote this reality. Admittedly I find that an odd term, but the image is useful. The righteousness that we have isn't something we possess or something we earn. It comes from outside of us. It's alien to our nature. It's imputed, or placed in, us. Paul describes this reality in Romans 5:19: "through the one man's obedience the many will be made righteous." This doesn't mean that through Jesus Christ, they will have a model for how to live a morally exemplary life. Instead, through faith in Jesus, they will be made (or declared) righteous. Those who were formally "in Adam" are now "in Christ," and the life He lived is credited to their account. Which means that the pressure is off. We don't have to earn righteousness, we can merely receive it as a gift.

How does the concept of imputed righteousness encourage you today?

_____

_____

_____

_____

_____

_____

_____

_____

_____

_____

_____

_____

_____

_____

_____

_____

DAY FORTY

We've all had a bad hair day (well, most of us)! You've rolled out of bed, sleepily made your way to the mirror, and wondered how you could face the day with the reflection staring back at you. Or maybe you've had the horror of a dinner party full of conversation and laughter that ends with a trip to the bathroom and a glance in the mirror only to see the hunk of lettuce stuck between your teeth. Not only are you embarrassed, but you know that lettuce is from the pre-meal salad so you've spent the last two hours looking like this.

READ JAMES 1:19-27

and notice how James says mirrors are supposed to help us.

_____

_____

_____

Mirrors are a gift. If you think it's bad news to have a bad hair day or a lettuce tooth, imagine what would happen if you didn't have a mirror. You would be left to go through life without any sense of what you look like. You have no way of seeing things that are out of whack in order to put them right.

Notice, however, the contrast James draws. There are two people mentioned in the passage. Both look into the mirror of God's truth. Both see what they look like in the reflection. But only one obeys and makes changes based on what he or she sees. The issue isn't that one has a mirror and the other doesn't. They both have the Word of God by which they can see what they look like. But only one is a "doer," the other is a "forgetful hearer" (v. 25).

Which are you? Are you the forgetful hearer or are you the faithful doer?

I think we'd all acknowledge the gift we have in the mirror of God's word. Much like the person with lettuce in their teeth, we'd be lost if we did not have a word from God to help us see who God is and who we are. Even more, there are many people around the world who do not have the word of God in their language. The word exists, but people can't read it. Most of us are richly blessed by comparison. Not only do we have God's word, but we also have it in our language, and we have many different translations and commentaries to help us understand God's word well. To stick to the image used in James, we have a massive mirror that is perfectly polished to help us see our reflection clearly.

James' observation, then, is critical for us. Since we have a spotless mirror, it's important that we take what we see in the mirror and translate it into action through our obedience, which is exactly what Solomon is exhorting the people of his day to do in Ecclesiastes 5. Since all of life under the sun is futile—money, possessions, wisdom, power—we should look beyond the sun for ultimate meaning. There we will find a God who has declared clearly what He expects from His people. He's given us a big mirror. And we should use it.

There are two implications that are immediately apparent. First, we have to be the kind of people who look into the mirror regularly. In the same way that you can't look in the mirror once a year or once a week, even, and have any sense of what you look like from day to day, neither can you merely look in the mirror of God's word in a sermon once a week and think that will be enough. You can't depend on what you saw in the mirror back in the day when you were committed to daily Bible reading. You have to look at the mirror regularly. The beauty of regular Bible reading is that God's Spirit will help you see different ideas and applications each time you look in the mirror of the Word. So we should come back to even familiar passages and ask God what He would want us to see.

Second, we have to act on what we see in the mirror. When we obey what we read, we train ourselves to do so the next time we come to the mirror. The more we look at God's word and adjust our beliefs and our lives to align with what we see there, the better prepared we will be to do the same in the future. Conversely, the more we read and fail to obey, the more we train ourselves to neglect the mirror in the future.

Let's end the week by taking some time to ask ourselves what God is showing us in His word right now that we need to obey.

_____

_____

_____

_____

_____

_____

_____

_____

_____

_____

_____

_____

_____

_____

_____

_____

WEEK
09

Folly

ECCLESIASTES
7:1-14; 10

"WISDOM IS AS GOOD
AS AN INHERITANCE
AND AN ADVANTAGE TO
THOSE WHO SEE THE SUN,
BECAUSE WISDOM IS
PROTECTION AS SILVER
IS PROTECTION; BUT
THE ADVANTAGE OF
KNOWLEDGEIS THAT
WISDOM PRESERVES
THE LIFE OF ITS OWNER."

ECCLESIASTES 7:11-12

"A KING WILL HAVE HIS
WAY IN HIS OWN HALL,
BE IT FOLLY OR WISDOM."

J.R.R. TOLKIEN,
THE TWO TOWERS

DAY FORTY-ONE

SCRIPTURE READING
Psalm 39:1-6

Funerals are the worst.[10] Even if you don't know the deceased person well, the events surrounding the death and burial of a person remind us of how unnatural death is. Death is sometimes described as an unwelcome intruder into our lives, and that's just what it feels like. Life is moving along at a steady pace, and then death breaks in and destroys everything.

One of the ways we know funerals are the worst is by the effort we take to reframe death. Sometimes you'll see funerals called a "Celebration of Life," an idea that attempts to shift the focus away from the horror of death and onto the beauty of a life well lived. There's nothing wrong with these sentiments, but there's something about the reality of death that we can't, and in fact we shouldn't, want to escape.

[10] This week's reflections are written by Matt Rogers, one of the pastors of Christ Fellowship Cherrydale in Greenville, South Carolina.

This week we are focusing on Ecclesiastes 7:1-14 and all of chapter 10. The first verses of this passage model the Psalmist's reflections in Psalm 29:1-6. Read that passage now and jot down some thoughts or questions you have about it.

_____

_____

_____

The Psalmist reminds us of the reality that makes funerals so uncomfortable: life is short. So, so short. Even for those who live what we might call full lives and make it into their 80s or 90s, it seems like a blink of an eye and they are gone. Perhaps you've experienced pictures popping up on your phone as a "memory," and been gripped by the swift passage of time. It seems like just yesterday when your kids were young, when you were newlyweds, or when you had hair! Like sand through an hourglass, time is passing and we can't seem to slow it down.

This is why Solomon could make the claims he does in Ecclesiastes 7. On the surface, his comments there seem odd: "It is better to go to a house of mourning than to go to a house of feasting, since that is the end of all mankind" (v. 2). No one wants to go to a house of mourning. Everyone is downtrodden. Tears replace laughter.

The house of feasting, on the other hand, is the place everyone wants to be! There's joy in this house. Loud voices. Fun stories. Food and drink. All the good things in life. If we were given a choice, most of us would always choose to go to the house of feasting rather than the house of mourning. But Solomon invites us to reconsider this choice. He says that we should prioritize the house of mourning. Why? Verse

2 tells us the answer. Death is the end of all mankind, and the house of mourning reminds us of this reality. When we are in the house of feasting, all we can think about is life. We assume that the joy and happiness we experience will last forever. We tend to forget about death. But in the house of mourning, death is all around. The wise person sees the house of mourning and takes the reality of death to heart.

What does it mean to take something to heart? The imagery is baked into the phrase. There's an idea that lies elsewhere, and we have to transport, or take, it to our hearts. Most often this work is moving something from your brain to your heart, and in this case, that is the exact transportation route. We know that life is short. Mentally this is clear. There's no debating the fact that we have fleeting lives. Even worse, we have no clue when those short lives will come to an end. Some are short, and others are even shorter. Finally, we know that our short lives aren't much more than a blip on the timeline of human history. If you want a super happy-clappy Psalm that makes this point, notice this ominous note from Psalm 103:

> As for man, his days are like grass —
> he blooms like a flower of the field;
> when the wind passes over it, it vanishes,
> and its place is no longer known (v. 15-16).

Thanks, David. Not only will I die, but now you're telling me that once I'm gone people aren't going to remember me for long. I'll vanish—both from this life and from the memories of others. But intellectually, as much as we'd like to repress these thoughts, we know they are true.

It's another thing, however, to allow these ideas to travel from your mind to your heart. This is a dangerous journey indeed, but it's one we must travel. And the house of mourning helps us here. The most realistic way for most of us to visit the house of mourning is by being involved in our local churches. There we will constantly be connected to people who are suffering and mourning. As we minister to them, we confront our fears of death and are better positioned to take death to heart.

> What would likely change about your life this week if
> you took death to heart in a more meaningful way?

_____

_____

_____

_____

_____

_____

_____

_____

_____

_____

_____

_____

DAY FORTY-TWO

If there's a defining cultural mantra in our day, it's hard to think of one more prominent than "Judge not!". This idea comes in many forms and expressions, but the general sentiment is that we should all just mind our own business. We should just let other people do their thing and not infringe on their individuality in any way, much less call something that they want to do a sin. In fact, it's ironic that there's no worse sin for most people than judgmentalism. It's an even bigger deal than whatever sin people are supposedly judging.

This cultural mantra flies in the face of the Bible's instruction for Christians, particularly how Christians are to interact with other Christians. While we should not be judgmental or condescending in our tone, the Bible is clear that Christians have a responsibility to

MATTERS OF THE HEART

confront other Christians when they sin (Matt 18:15-20). This doesn't mean that we are to walk around our city looking for any professing Christian to rebuke. Rather, in the context of the family of the local church, we should strive to love our brothers and sisters by having restorative conversations when they sin.

READ MATTHEW 18:15-20.

What do you observe about Jesus' instructions here?

_____

_____

_____

Have you ever had someone come to you and express hurt long after they felt offended? For example, you notice that someone is distant or frustrated but you can't put your finger on why, and then some two or three years later, they admit that you did something in the past that rubbed them the wrong way or hurt their feelings. If you have, then you are most likely to say, "Why didn't you tell me then?" We don't want people to hold an issue against us for years and not give us the chance to talk about it or make things right.

How about the situation where you see someone blow up his or her life or family with gross immorality. Maybe you've sat on the couch in someone's living room and listened to them weep over a recent affair and a pending divorce. If so, it's likely that there were signs that things weren't right leading up to this moment. A stray word. A demeaning tone in conversation. An admission of pornography struggles. Crass jokes in public. Now the sin has taken hold, and the damage is done.

201

"Why didn't you stop me sooner?", the person will often ask on the back end of their failure. "If you saw the issues and you knew the pain that was coming, why didn't you speak up and help me get out before it was too late?"

These are the situations Matthew 18 is addressing—sin among Christians, especially in the church. There's a normative pathway outlined in this passage. This is not meant to be a legalistic, step 1, step 2 process; rather, it's the guiding principles that inform how we respond.

First, we go to the person directly. We don't talk to other people about the issue. We don't harbor bitterness for the wrongs they've done. We don't rehearse in our minds how we might get even. We do the hard thing of speaking up and saying what's really going on. Now, we might not always know exactly what's going on. We don't have to come with an accusatory tone. Sometimes it might be that we say something like, "Hey brother, I'm not sure all that's going on, but when you speak to your wife or about your wife in a small group, it sure seems that you are not honoring her as you should. Is everything ok?" or "Friend, I've noticed that you seem to be checked out in church worship and small groups. Is everything ok with your walk with the Lord right now?" Of course, there are other times when we need to be more direct. If we've witnessed a person's sin or they've clearly sinned against us then it's appropriate to speak clearly about the wrong that's been done.

Then involve another person or two. This is the path only if the first doesn't work. No need to involve anyone else if the brother or sister repents and seeks forgiveness. But if not, take another person with you—maybe a mutual friend or someone in the small group—and widen the circle of accountability.

Finally, involve the church and its leaders. Bring the pastors of the church into the issue. These should be mature men who will not gossip about the situation. They should be able to help you seek restoration, adjudicate wrongs that have been done, and mediate hard conversations that need to be resolved. The final stage of informing the church is a case of blatant disregard for sin and holiness. The person is clearly in the wrong, doesn't care, and pledges to persist in their waywardness. In such a case, we are instructed to act and interact with them as if they were not believers in Jesus at all because their actions are not giving indication of their conversion.

More can be said about the last step, but notice where it all begins. Healthy conflict in the church occurs when Christians do hard things and seek out the wayward for the sake of restoring them to God and to right relationship with the church.

Where do you need to practice Matthew 18 this week?

_____

_____

_____

_____

_____

_____

_____

_____

DAY FORTY-THREE

SCRIPTURE READING
Philippians 4:10-14

Let's be honest—the opening of Ecclesiastes 7 is filled with hard truth like this idea from verse 14: "In the day of prosperity be joyful, but in the day of adversity, consider: God has made the one as well as the other, so that no one can discover anything that will come after him."

READ PHILIPPIANS 4:10-14.

What is the dominant theme of this paragraph?

_____

_____

_____

Contentment.

There's a reason Jeremiah Burroughs titled his book *The Rare Jewel of Christian Contentment*. Contentment is a rare jewel indeed. And before we move on, if you haven't read Burroughs' book then you should order it now so you can start it as soon as you finish this devotion. Once you work through some of the old English, the themes of the book are instructive, convincing, and compelling.

In the context of Philippians 4, Paul is writing to churches who are supporting him in his missionary work. It's not all been a glowing victory lap for Paul—he's faced difficulty upon difficulty. You know the drill—ship wrecks, snake bites, opposition from enemies. In Philippians 4, Paul isn't talking about these things so much as he's talking about the financial resources for his ventures. He's dependent upon the support of these churches to do the work. But he doesn't want to invite them to a pity party like, "If you don't support me then I won't have food to eat or ways to get from city to city and I might die." In the era before Venmo, Grubhub, Uber, and Yelp, such a claim might be true. If these churches didn't send resources to Paul, then he was a dead man.

Paul chooses a different approach that is surely representative of his heart. He tells the church that he's good. He's learned to be content. If he has much, then great. Praise God. If he doesn't have much. Fine.

This language models the wisdom of Solomon in Ecclesiastes 7 where he encourages joy in both prosperity and adversity. Why? Because God has ordained both.

None of us are predisposed to be content. In fact, it's just the opposite. Watch a young child interact with the world, and you'll notice that his or her primary impulse is to be discontent. One night we were watching a family movie. It was my 4-year-old's night to pick the movie. No more than 20 minutes after the movie started, he came to me and said, "Daddy, can I go watch my own movie on your iPad?" He was discontent with the movie he'd picked out for the family to watch! Such is the pattern for children, whether food or movies or toys or games or friends or fun. We tend to want what we don't have, even if what we have is pretty good.

Wouldn't it be great if we grew out of discontentment as adults? It isn't easy to stop wanting what you don't have all the time. Even when you get it you find out that you want something else more. It's a vicious cycle, and it demands that we ask a hard question of ourselves: when will I have enough?

Financially, you can find countless online tools that intend to give you an exact dollar amount to answer this question. If you have x-amount of money at a certain age, then your net worth tells us that you can retire and live on this money for the rest of your life. With inflation numbers as they are, this number tends to keep changing and growing and the projected amount necessitates a life-long pursuit of enough. So, then, is it possible for a person in their 30s or 40s to have enough? Take it out of the realm of pure dollars and cents for a minute. Can you have a big enough house? Enough vacation? A good enough church? Enough friends? Enough meaningful work to do? If the answer to these questions is always "no" then we have a massive problem. We can't ever be content. If enough is always predicated on some future place or position, then we can never realize contentment in the present.

There's a necessary tension here, right? We have meaningful work to do. We need to save and spend our money well. We should consider how to use our resources in our retirement years. We should care about making our churches and our families better. But perhaps more of us need to be challenged to stop and take in all that God is doing and has done in our life. Whether in joy or sorrow, to stop and itemize the blessings we've received. This practice is more than simply stopping to smell the roses from time to time. It's a radical orientation to life that isn't constantly grappling for more. And it's a good way to live.

Where do you need to pursue contentment today?

_____

_____

_____

_____

_____

_____

_____

_____

_____

DAY FORTY-FOUR

If you look up the words "wisdom" and "folly" in the Bible, you will find that a majority of the times these words are used, they are in the books of Proverbs or Ecclesiastes. You might go so far as to suggest that the main goal of these books is to outline God's path to wisdom or God's plan to avoid folly. Like the sheep and goats in Jesus' stories, Solomon breaks the world into two kinds of people—those who are wise and those who are fools.

Today's passage is from the end of the Sermon on the Mount.

confront other Christians when they sin (Matt 18:15-20). This doesn't mean that we are to walk around our city looking for any professing Christian to rebuke. Rather, in the context of the family of the local church, we should strive to love our brothers and sisters by having restorative conversations when they sin.

READ MATTHEW 7:24-29

and notice how Jesus speaks of wisdom
and folly in this passage.

You've probably seen it happen. You go to the beach and notice a kid embarking on building the world's greatest sand castle. They dig the moat, build the foundation, and start adding details to their architectural wonder. But there's a problem—they started building the castle at low tide and underestimated how far the waves would come in when the tides changed. But by this point it's too late. There's only a matter of time before a wave takes out their hours of work.

The same happens with houses built along the coast. What once was a sure foundation for new homes has eroded over time. Now, even the stilt-extended homes are one bad storm away from being washed out to the sea.

Life is like this, Jesus says. There are foolish builders who build their lives on a poor foundation, a sandy foundation. Other builders—the wise ones—build on a rock. Here Jesus is likely making two points. First, He is communicating that He is the Rock. He is the only foundation worthy of our lives. And, He is communicating that His truth is a rock. Wise people build their lives on the truth of His word.

The test comes when the storm rolls in. Up to that point, it's virtually impossible to tell the difference between the wise and foolish builder. But when the wind and the waves and the rain start, it becomes quite obvious whose house is on the sand and whose is on the rock. Once the storm arrives, you can't change the foundation of the building any more than you can move a sandcastle once the tide shifts.

Which means that, like the wise builder, we have to determine where we will build in pleasant conditions so that we are prepared for the approaching storm. The storms will come, this much is certain. Our foundation will be tested.

Is the foundation of your life built on Christ and His word?

It can be hard to answer that question with confidence. We may know that we trusted Christ at one point in our journey, but how can we be sure where our foundation is now?

This is where suffering and pain helps us. The storms reveal the foundation. Peter makes this point in his first letter: "You rejoice in this, even though now for a short time, if necessary, you suffer grief in various trials so that the proven character of your faith — more valuable than gold which, though perishable, is refined by fire — may result in praise, glory, and honor at the revelation of Jesus Christ" (1 Pet. 1:6-7). Notice the phrase "proven character of your faith" Our faith (and I think we could rightly substitute "our foundation") must be proven. It must be tested. Suffering does this for us. We can't test the foundation well ourselves, so God sends storms into our lives that help us see where and how we are building.

You may be walking through some hard things right now. You've likely gone through something hard in recent memory. Think about that suffering and ask yourself: What am I learning about my foundation when I suffer? The wind and the waves help us see things about our hearts and minds that we would not otherwise be able to see. This is the gift of suffering. The only way we can rejoice in suffering is to know that it is doing something in us that we could not, or would not, get to on our own.

**What are the difficulties and suffering in your
life revealing about your foundation?**

_____

_____

_____

_____

_____

_____

_____

_____

_____

_____

DAY FORTY-FIVE

SCRIPTURE READING

Titus 3:4-11

The Bible claims to describe and define the path of wisdom. Solomon includes a number of proverbial wisdom sayings within the book of Ecclesiastes, but in essence the entirety of the book is a claim about wisdom. Wise people understand that all of life is futile, chasing after the wind. The Bible's authors, however, understood that there would always be those who professed to speak on God's behalf, and there would be those who lead others into folly.

READ TITUS 3:4-11.

What do you notice about Paul's warning here?

_____

_____

_____

The popular show *MythBusters* capitalized on the propensity of humans to get swept away by foolish beliefs. The show takes and tests popular notions to see if, in fact, they are true. What makes the show is just how many of these commonly held "truths" aren't actually true. For example:

→ Can a heavy insect hitting a motorcycle rider in the right spot actually kill the rider?

→ Would a penny dropped from a skyscraper gain enough speed to kill someone walking below?

→ Is it possible for an avalanche to be caused by someone yodeling?

Granted, these examples are silly, right? Our lives are not likely to be impacted by a penny falling off of a skyscraper (pun intended). Even popular myths like the existence of the Loch Ness monster, aliens, or Bigfoot don't shape the lives of ordinary people (except those super cool guys who hunt for Bigfoot in the Pacific Northwest).

These examples do reveal the human propensity to get sucked into myths, though. Paul commends the church in Crete, where Titus is the pastor, to give themselves fully to good works and not get lost in "foolish debates, genealogies, quarrels, and disputes about the law" (Titus 3:9).

Other translations use "silly myths" in place of "foolish debates." Now, these early Christians weren't getting sucked into the type of myths that would likely show up on MythBusters. They were easily swept away by endless speculation about philosophical concepts that had nothing to do with the gospel of Jesus Christ. In that day, the high water mark of human virtue was to be seen as a wise person. Wisdom was the peak of human existence. So, to get to that place, people would spend endless time bantering about the intricacies of speculative philosophy or try to make sense of life based on family genealogies, and they would fuss and fight with others over whose interpretation was right.

Paul told them to stop all that. You might say that Paul says here that there is a foolish way to try to be wise. Or that in trying to be wise, or make oneself look wise to others, a person can actually be a fool. Our modern era is different, but the same. We may not debate the same concepts that first century philosophers did, but we are no less apt to get lost in endless speculation about concepts that the Bible has little to say about or that do little to change our pursuit of the good works that God has called us to.

One way to discern godly wisdom from silly myths is to notice the truth that the Bible is clear on. When we read the Bible, God is abundantly clear on the nature of sin, the need for salvation, the work of Jesus Christ, and salvation through faith. But the Bible isn't as clear on the exact mechanics of all of that good news. There's complexity and tension that we have to embrace. For example, God is fully in charge of all things and knows the end from the beginning but he tells us to pray. Or, God ordains and allows sin but doesn't tempt us to sin. There's complexity there that we can't deny. But then again, the Bible is also clear about how we are called to obey Him in many areas. For example, we are told that husbands are to love their wives as Christ did the church, that parents are to raise children in the love and admonition of the Lord, that we should redeem our lives and use our time for doing good, or that our bodies are temples of God. However, the Bible doesn't provide all that you need to know about dating or courtship, it doesn't give a one-size-fits-all parenting philosophy, it doesn't tell you how to go about choosing a career, and it doesn't provide a dietary plan or exercise regime.

So we want to pursue wisdom in the areas that God is clear on and use that wisdom to guide our decisions in areas that the Bible isn't as clear on. However, as we apply sanctified wisdom to these other areas, we must be careful that we don't get sucked into silliness. I think there's clear guidance for us in Titus 3. Notice the connection that Paul makes between these controversial and speculative matters and quarrels and debates. We may be able to tell when we've crossed the line when our views on various matters make us divisive. It's important that we have the wisdom to 1) have firm convictions on our theology and practice and 2) recognize that there are other Christians who see things differently than you do in that area. Wise Christians know how to balance conviction and charity. To do so doesn't mean we are compromising on the gospel—it shows that we have the wisdom to know what is a first-level gospel issue and what isn't, and it helps us avoid getting swept away by endless speculation.

Where do you need to grow in conviction and/or charitability?

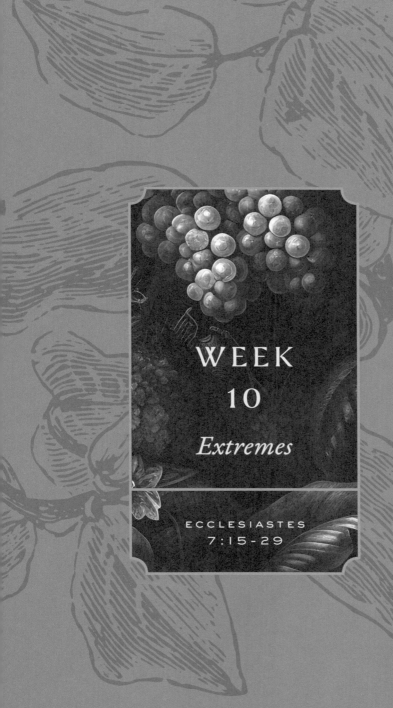

WEEK

10

Extremes

ECCLESIASTES
7:15-29

"ONLY SEE THIS: I HAVE
DISCOVERED THAT
GOD MADE PEOPLE
UPRIGHT, BUT THEY
PURSUED MANY
SCHEMES."

ECCLESIASTES 7:9

"LIFE IS LIKE RIDING
A BICYCLE. TO KEEP
YOUR BALANCE, YOU
MUST KEEP MOVING."

ALBERT EINSTEIN

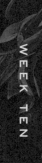

DAY FORTY-SIX

SCRIPTURE READING
Psalm 73

We all want a certain arithmetic to work out in life.[11] Do good and get good in return. Do evil and get paid back with something worse. We think it would be nice if life worked with this level of predictability.

But we know it doesn't work this way, in our lives or in the lives of others. It's bad enough when we think we've done good and get bad in return. But what about those who do evil and seem to have a good life? This is the question the Psalmist asks in Psalm 73.

[11]This week's reflections are written by Matt Rogers, one of the pastors of Christ Fellowship Cherrydale in Greenville, South Carolina.

READ PSALM 73

and note what emotions are expressed there and why.

_____

_____

_____

_____

One of the reasons I love the Bible is the raw honesty it expresses. What Asaph says in Psalm 73 isn't something most of us would be comfortable saying, much less writing down for others to read. He's frustrated by the good life the wicked are living. They "have an easy time... their bodies are well fed...they are not afflicted" (v. 4-5).

We might not express our frustration publicly, but we've surely felt something like this. We watch as the person who lies, cheats, and steals to get ahead actually succeeds. We notice a serial adulterer enjoying a relaxing vacation with his newest wife. We see those who bail on Jesus and the church live it up on social media.

We contrast these images with our own lives. We've sacrificially given our money to God's mission and do not have the funds for luxurious vacations. We have persevered in marriage for decades, even when it's hard, and chosen to forgive and pursue our spouse. We've chosen the hard and narrow way, yet we experience suffering and difficulty. The arithmetic doesn't seem to add up.

If we were evaluating God like we might a parent, we'd have to conclude that something was out of whack. What parent would want to reward the kid who does wrong and discipline the child who is compliant? It's easy to "become embittered" and find our "innermost being was wounded" when we assess God's justice in this life.

And "this life" is the key. If we look at this life, we will see many examples of inequity. However, God is not constrained to this life like we are. His just judgment for humans is largely seen from an eternal perspective. At the end of human history, God will settle all scores (Rev. 21:5-8). The believer's merit will not be through his or her good works, but through faith in the perfect righteousness of Christ given as a free gift (Eph. 2:1-10). The unbeliever, however, will be held accountable for his or her unrighteousness when confronted with the perfect holiness of God. They will be judged, even if, in this life, it appeared they had gotten away with their folly.

The knowledge of the final judgment helps us balance extremes in this life. We can, and should, want to point out the errors of those living apart from God's design. We shouldn't merely put our head in the sand and pretend like their sin doesn't exist. We should be willing to call sin, sin, and invite our neighbors, coworkers, family, and friends to turn from that sin and trust in Christ.

But we must not lose heart when things go well for these people. We should not resent, envy, or seek to destroy them. We should not gossip behind their backs or mock their folly. We also should not give up on doing good in our own lives because it seems that God isn't rewarding us the way that we think He should.

We can join with the Psalmist in expressing: "You guide me with your counsel, and afterward you will take me up in glory. Who do I have in heaven but you? And I desire nothing on earth but you" (Ps. 73:24-25). The contrast here is clear—I'm not guided by my frustrations with the wicked, I'm not compelled to give up or seek the easy life. Rather, I'm guided by God's counsel alone. I choose to trust that His ways are best even if that doesn't seem to be the case based on what I can see.

Furthermore, my desire is Him. I don't desire the life of ease that the wicked have. I want God, not the trinkets that this world has to offer. Like the man who finds a treasure hidden in a field, I am willing to sell all else because God and His kingdom are my great reward (Matt 13:44-46).

**Where do you find yourself most tempted
to envy the lives of the wicked?**

_____

_____

_____

_____

_____

_____

_____

_____

_____

_____

DAY FORTY-SEVEN

SCRIPTURE READING

Deuteronomy 8:11-20

There's a real sense in which the whole of the book of Ecclesiastes describes balance in life. On the one hand, Solomon says that everything is fleeting and futile, like chasing after the wind (Ecc. 1:2, 2:11). On the other hand, he also writes: "So I commended enjoyment because there is nothing better for a person under the sun than to eat, drink, and enjoy himself, for this will accompany him in his labor during the days of his life that God gives him under the sun" (Ecc. 8:15).

You likely don't remember your first time riding a bicycle, but odds are you've still got a few scrapes and scars from your attempts.

Once it clicks, riding a bike is fairly easy, but at the start it's a real challenge for most. You have to find that point of balance. A little too much to the right or left and you will crash. And you have to maintain that balance even if you go around a sharp curve or have to stop suddenly. Balance is difficult to find, much less maintain.

READ DEUTERONOMY 8:11-20.

What does this passage have to do with balance?

_____

_____

_____

It's interesting that balance doesn't come by hyper-focusing on balance itself. We don't succeed in riding a bike by spending time thinking about balance. In the same way, we don't drive a car straight by gripping the steering wheel as tightly as we can. The more you ride a bike or drive a car, the more comfortable you get at finding the needed balance to simply enjoy the ride.

Balance in life doesn't come through focusing on balance either. Balance is found in focusing on God and His word. The language of Deuteronomy 8 is framed in the negative. Don't forget. Don't forget God. Don't forget His Word. Don't forget what He's done for you. Don't forget the critical role of obedience.

Spun positively, we could say—Remember God. Remember God's Word. Remember what He's done for you. Remember how important it is to obey.

You have to tell someone to remember because they are prone to forget. This was true for the people in Moses' day. This was the very nation that had been freed from slavery in Egypt, miraculously delivered through the Red Sea, brought safely through decades of wandering in the wilderness, and brought to stand on the brink of the Promised Land. If they were tempted to forget God, how much more so are we?

We tend to forget God for the very reasons Solomon warns against in the book of Ecclesiastes. There's so much going on in our lives—people, money, work, wisdom, power, influence, need. We know it's all fleeting, but these themes tend to be front and center in our hearts and minds each day. It's dizzying.

I tend to get motion sickness, especially if I'm riding in the back seat of a car or on a boat. The key to avoiding sickness, I've come to learn, is to focus on a fixed point on the horizon. If I fix my attention on what's right in front of me—the boat bobbing in the waves or the trees flashing by in the car window, then I'm doomed. But if I can find a point in the distance that stays fixed even though the things right in front of me are moving, then I can survive.

We find balance in life by fixing our attention on God. Our world makes us motion sick merely by living in it. We get out of balance easily. Sometimes we idolize the money or the power or the wisdom that gets us out of balance. Other times, we get out of balance simply by living in a world where those realities exist; we have to consider money, schedules, parenting, marriage, jobs, emails, text messages, dirty dishes, laundry, dating, decisions, Covid, politics, race, frustrations with a neighbor, brake issues in the car, college planning...Right? The list is never-ending. Many of these things you can't avoid, even if you aren't idolizing them. But if you focus on them, they will throw you off balance.

It sounds easy to say that we should focus on God. But it's the simple key to living in a world that makes us motion sick.

How would you evaluate your focus right now?

_____

_____

_____

_____

_____

_____

_____

_____

_____

_____

_____

_____

_____

_____

_____

DAY FORTY-EIGHT

SCRIPTURE READING

Proverbs 4:20-27

What was the world like before the days of cell phone maps? Some may remember the days of printing out directions or attempting to follow a huge, laminated map to get from one place or another. Now we have the little voice chirping in our cars telling us when to turn, where to turn, and exactly how far we have until that turn arrives. We just need to listen to the voice and follow what the voice says.

READ PROVERBS 4:20-27.

What do you notice about the directions given there?

_____

_____

_____

Solomon is giving his son encouragement on the path of wisdom, and he says to fix your eyes straight ahead. He urges his son to not even look to the right or the left, much less move in one of those directions. In this passage, Solomon is providing the path through His wise counsel. By way of expansion, we can rightly suggest that the totality of God's word is the path to life and wisdom. Not merely the book of Proverbs but all of the Holy Scriptures. As Paul says in 2 Timothy 3:

> All Scripture is inspired by God and is profitable for teaching, for rebuking, for correcting, for training in righteousness, so that the man of God may be complete, equipped for every good work (v. 16-17).

God's people, those in the path of wisdom, stay focused on God's word. These words guide and direct both their ultimate life trajectory and their final destination.

We should not read the idea of turning "to the right or to the left" (Prov. 3:27) through the lens of contemporary, political banter, as if "turning to the left" were a move toward liberalism and "to the right" were a warning against fundamentalism. The point is simply to stay focused on God's word and not to devitate.

Notice the connection to the heart in verse 23. Typically, this verse is used in connection with modern dating. "Guard your heart" by not falling in love with someone too soon. That's certainly an implication of the concept of staying true to God's word, but the point here is that the primary way that we guard our hearts is by obeying all of God's truth. The closer we seek to align ourselves with God's word, the more likely our hearts will be protected from evil and harm.

There are countless ways that we turn to the right or the left from God's word, but let's consider a reason that lies at the root. We tend to turn from God's wisdom because we trust in our wisdom. The book of Proverbs warns against this temptation: "Trust in the Lord with all your heart, and do not rely on your own understanding; in all your ways know him, and he will make your paths straight" (Prov. 3:5-6). When we rely on our own understanding, we swerve to the right or the left.

The Bible presses us in many ways. We simply can't go through life without wisdom. We face challenges that are complex. It would be awesome if the issues we face were clean cut, black or white issues, but they aren't. Many of the issues are gray. Not only that, the Bible doesn't speak to every issue we face. This doesn't mean that the Bible isn't sufficient for the issues we face, but it does mean that it's not composed as a clean list of "*20 Steps to Parent Teenagers*" or "*30 Ways to Rebuild a Marriage after an Affair*" or "*The Playbook for Navigating Mental Health Issues in the Family*" or "*Surefire Ways to Make a Career Change in Your 40s.*" The Bible's wisdom guides us in these issues, but it's not neat and tidy. We have to take wisdom we find in the Word, ask the Spirit for help and direction, and make sanctified decisions about the issues we face. All this takes work. It takes a commitment to God's word. We have to read the Bible, understand what it means, and apply it to the complexity we face. Work is hard, as we all know. The temptation is to shortcut the process and do what Proverbs warns against, to "lean on our own understanding."

The word picture of leaning is instructive for us. Think about a time when you've leaned against a table or a stool. If you are really leaning against an object, you are putting your weight on it. If it gives out, if one of the legs breaks, or if it shifts under your weight, then you will fall. You are depending on what you lean on for strength and support.

So what are you leaning on right now?

Are you leaning on your own wisdom or God's?

How do you know?

DAY FORTY-NINE

SCRIPTURE READING
James 3:1-12

"Sticks and stones may break your bones,
but words will never hurt me."

Has there ever been a more ridiculous statement?

READ JAMES 3:1-12.

What does James tell us about the power of words?

_____

_____

_____

We've likely heard and experienced the warning that James gives here. Today, I want us to consider what happens when the fire of the untamed tongue begins to spread. The writer of James agrees with Solomon that the mouth often spews curses. Notice how Solomon warns those on the receiving end of these curses: "Don't pay attention to everything people say, or you may hear your servant cursing you, for in your heart you know that many times you yourself have cursed others" (Ecc. 7:21-22).

This is easier said than done. Our natural impulse is to curse right back at those who curse us. Not only does Solomon say that we should not curse in return, he says that we should simply ignore those who are cursing us. The motive given is that we've all cursed others, and we know how foolish our tongues have been in the past. Solomon urges that we give people the benefit of the doubt. We should move through our lives without giving undue attention to what others say. The implication from Solomon's warning is that we should listen to what others say, whether it's good or bad. We don't need to give undue attention to those who might inflame our pride or those who might tear us down.

So what should you do when you hear someone curse you? This might be actual cursing, or it could be those who tear you down, lie about you, or aim to harm you with their words. Peter suggests that the cursing of others gives us a chance to act like Jesus:

> For you were called to this, because Christ also suffered for you, leaving you an example, that you should follow in his steps. He did not commit sin, and no deceit was found in his mouth; when he was insulted, he did not insult in return; when he suffered, he did not threaten but entrusted himself to the one who judges justly (1 Pet. 2:21-23).

Jesus' model here is compelling because he actually had the right to fight back. He was innocent of the charges against Him. He was perfect. All of the accusations were bogus.

And Jesus had the power to get even. Had He chosen to do so, He could have leveled His enemies and enacted immediate justice against those doing Him harm. We can't say the same things about ourselves. We don't have the purity or the power Jesus has. We are sinners and we know it. So when others say sinful things to us or about us, we often say sinful things in return. Even if we've matured, when we look back on our past we know that we've often thrown punches when people have hurt us. We also lack the power to do anything about the harm others do. We can't right the wrongs that are done to us. We are not in the position to execute perfect justice. When we have power, we tend to use it to crush others or do harm to them in return.

How much more, then, should we follow Jesus' example? Since we don't have the purity or the power to get even with those who curse us, we shouldn't be as concerned with those who do so in the first place. Granted, this is easier said than done. The sticks and stones of others' words really do hurt. They can break us, especially if we give them too much time and attention. Solomon is wise to remind us to avoid listening to what others say about us in the first place. The less we hear, the less we consider, and the less we are tempted to take to heart.

Start today by thinking about the negative words that have impacted you recently. Maybe it's the words of a spouse, a child, or a close family member that have brought harm. Maybe you've had a coworker turn on you and undermine you. Maybe you had a friend who stabbed you in the back, lied about you, or is seeking to do you harm. Rather than stewing in bitterness, admit to God the harm these words have done. Ask Him to give you the grace and forgiveness to overlook an offense and, rather than returning evil for evil, do good instead. Consider Peter's reminder:

> Finally, all of you be like-minded and sympathetic, love one another, and be compassionate and humble, not paying back evil for evil or insult for insult but, on the contrary, giving a blessing, since you were called for this, so that you may inherit a blessing. For the one who wants to love life and to see good days, let him keep his tongue from evil and his lips from speaking deceit, and let him turn away from evil and do what is good. Let him seek peace and pursue it, because the eyes of the Lord are on the righteous and his ears are open to their prayer. But the face of the Lord is against those who do what is evil (1 Pet. 3:8-12).

Where do you need to obey this passage today?

DAY FIFTY

There's another tension expressed in Ecclesiastes 7 when Solomon writes: "I have discovered that God made people upright, but they pursued many schemes" (v. 29). There are two facets of humanity mentioned here: 1) the glory of God's created design and 2) the horror of human sin. Both realities are clearly taught and demonstrated throughout the Bible's story, and it's important for us to avoid overstating either of these realities at the expense of the other. Humans are both gloriously created and deeply broken.

READ PSALM 8.

Which of these aspects of humans does the Psalmist note here?

_____

_____

_____

Churches, denominations, and leaders are prone to hyperfocus on either human worth or human sin. It's easy to notice the first group—those who focus on human worth and self-esteem without acknowledging and teaching the doctrine of the depravity of man. Much of the self-esteem movement in our day is built around those who focus too much on the person's dignity and not enough on their sinfulness.

But the opposite error can happen as well. Sometimes when we hyperfocus on sin, we either intentionally or unintentionally communicate that the only defining trait of humans is their sin.

Think about this tendency embodied in a parent. The dad only sees his son's sinfulness and speaks often about what the boy is doing wrong. He's quick to critique and chastise. Discipline is common. Try as he might, the son cannot seem to do anything to please his dad. This type of parenting can crush children, who learn to identify themselves by their worst actions. Over time, the child might cower in shame and guilt, lash out in anger, or simply rebel against his or her parents as a way of escaping the disdain experienced in the home.

If we're not careful, we can move through life equating this type of parental philosophy with God's interactions with us. We picture Him with a perpetual scowl, always disappointed in what we are doing or what we should be doing but aren't. He's an angry father looking to crush us with discipline at the first opportunity.

Psalm 8 reminds us that God sees dignity, worth, and value in those that He made. We are not just our sin. We are the beloved creation of a perfect God who made us to reflect His glory in the world (Gen. 1:26-28). Psalm 8 says that humans are made a little lower than God, which is a pretty lofty position (v. 5). Because this is true, people have glory and honor (v. 5). Notice that this glory and honor doesn't come from what we do. It's not something we earn through good behavior or lose when we sin. We have glory and honor simply by virtue of the fact that God made us and chose to give us a unique role in His world. Unlike the animals or the trees or the oceans, we have the capacity to know God and relate to Him in a personal way. On the scale of creation, humans are at the top of the list. As the Psalmist writes: "You made him ruler over the works of your hands; you put everything under his feet" (Ps. 8:6). This claim replicates the task that God gave Adam and Eve in the Garden when they were instructed to rule over the world God made (Gen. 1:26). God communicates the worth He sees in people by giving them this role as representatives of His rule and reign over all of creation. What a glorious privilege!

The fact that God sees us like this actually compels us to serve Him. Again, parenting is a case study here. Often, what kids need most isn't merely a parent who enforces the rules, but one who envelops them in love. They need someone who can discipline them when they've erred, but who can do so with a view toward restoration and wholeness, not merely punishment. Study after study shows that children thrive in two parent homes where the parents love each other faithfully and seek to extend that love to their children. When love isn't present, kids often act out simply in an effort to find someone who will validate them or give them the attention they craved from their parents in the first place.

The same pattern happens in churches. The pulpit should talk about both the created glory of men and women and their overwhelming depravity. When pastors merely crush people with judgment over sin, it can have the opposite effect to what they want. People aren't compelled to obey a God out of guilt alone. They also need a high view of the love of God and the value and worth He has given each of them. That love then compels us to want to obey Him.

How does the love of God motivate your worship today?

WEEK

11

Enjoy

ECCLESIASTES 9

"Go, eat your bread with pleasure, and drink your wine with a cheerful heart, for God has already accepted your works. Let your clothes be white all the time, and never let oil be lacking on your head. Enjoy life with the wife you love all the days of your fleeting life, which has been given to you under the sun, all your fleeting days. For that is your portion in life and in your struggle under the sun. Whatever your hands find to do, do with all your strength, because there is no work, planning, knowledge, or wisdom in Sheol where you are going."

ECCLESIASTES 3:19

"The marvelous richness of human experience would lose something of rewarding joy if there were no limitations to overcome. The hilltop hour would not be half so wonderful if there were no dark valleys to traverse."

HELEN KELLER

DAY FIFTY-ONE

SCRIPTURE READING
Job 21:7-34

Have you ever received an answer to a question that made you regret asking the question in the first place?[12] A child might ask his parents what a particular noise was, even though the child may not really want the answer to that question. As we uncover the realities of our sin-stained world, we gain wisdom that sobers us and better equips us to engage the brokenness we find. With great wisdom comes great sobriety.

By chapter 21 of the book, Job was suffering. He had suddenly lost his children, been betrayed by his wife, and afflicted with sores from head to toe. From the depths of his grief, he ponders lofty truths about life with three "friends" as they discuss the reason for his tragedies.

[12] This week's reflections are written by Leonard Pisano, a member of Christ Fellowship Cherrydale in Greenville, South Carolina.

READ JOB 21:7-34.

What do you observe about this passage?

_____

_____

_____

_____

Job stumbles upon Solomon-like wisdom when he says:

> One person dies in excellent health,
> completely secure and at ease.
> His body is well fed,
> and his bones are full of marrow.
> Yet another person dies with a bitter soul,
> having never tasted prosperity.
> But they both lie in the dust,
> and worms cover them (v. 22-26).

It is easy to imagine why Job sounded so depressed. Though he had done nothing explicitly wrong to earn his hardships, he was experiencing them nonetheless. If we read between the lines, we can also imagine Job wishing for just one more meaningful moment with his children. It would be a reasonable human reaction. We, like Job, often underestimate how fortunate we are until the blessings we experience are removed. The reason we must value every moment we are alive is because, as Job realized: life and death are completely unpredictable.

Solomon often embodied the reality that with the blessings of knowledge and wisdom come sobriety. If that was not clear already, he opens chapter nine of Ecclesiastes with wisdom that aligns with Job's words: everybody dies. Solomon is the king of heavy wisdom. Solomon was not just having a bad day, like Job, though. He recognized the beauty in life's brevity. Solomon realized that though death is unpredictable and inevitable, this does not void life of its meaning and purpose. Simple supply and demand economics tell us that scarcity causes value. Unlike Job in the moment of his desolation, we are not left with these bleak realizations without a bright side. None of us know how much life we have left, and this makes us value the hours we are given and, hopefully, spring to action.

What would you do if you found out the world was going to end next Monday morning?

_____

_____

_____

I am a hopeless optimist. Even in the hardest seasons of life, I like to speak about life in a positive tone and focus on my blessings. Negative emotions make me uncomfortable. Watching the seconds on the clock tick by one at a time makes me question if I am utilizing my time to the best of my ability. So this message about death is hard for me. But James echoes Job and Solomon by reminding us, "Yet you do not know what tomorrow will bring—what your life will be! For you are like vapor that appears for a little while, then vanishes" (Jam. 4:14).

I can't help but read Ecclesiastes 9 without honestly questioning, "Do I really need to keep this in mind?" Hear me out, there is great value in focusing on God's goodness to us, but I am still tempted to minimize the sober and sad realities in life. Thinking about the end of my life is not a practice I enjoy. Although challenging, I think we can benefit from remembering the brevity of life as we seek to honor the Lord in all we do.

When we fully embrace our inability to control the outcome of our lives, we can find greater joy in God's blessings to us. As C.T. Studd, the famous British missionary, so beautifully wrote, "Only one life, 'twill soon be past, Only what's done for Christ will last." Therefore, we cannot put obedience off for tomorrow when the Lord has called us to it today.

> **What have you been putting off for later**
> **that the Lord has called you to now?**

DAY FIFTY-TWO

Few phrases are sweeter to the despairing ear than Solomon's words in Ecclesiastes 9: "...There is hope" (v. 4). You may not despair when you remember the brevity of life, but all of us have felt some sense of despair from time to time.

Jesus taught "If anyone wants to follow after me, let him deny himself, take up his cross, and follow me" (Matt.16:24). As we follow Jesus' example, we can count on hardships that may make us question if our mission is worth it. Sometimes, those hardships may make us ask if life is even worth living. In any case, the words in Hebrews and Isaiah offer us hopeful wisdom for life. There is hope! Remember how fatalistic Job's words were yesterday? Solomon's observation that brevity and unpredictability bring value to life is some consolation for those who experience anxiety over death, but a far superior hope still remains for those who are in Christ!

Recall a situation or experience that made you despair. What were you worried about? Then, recall a situation where good news helped you press on through tough circumstances. What hope did the good news give you?

_____

_____

_____

_____

In most cases, it is more advantageous to be a lion than a dog. At the time that Solomon wrote this analogy in Ecclesiastes 9, the lion was considered the king of the animal kingdom, while the dog was considered a beggar, waiting for scraps. How can being a begging dog ever be considered more desirable than being a kingly lion?

Solomon, clearly, had a change of heart. In Ecclesiastes 4:2, he had commended the dead over the living. Just a few chapters ago, he considered death more meaningful than life. The futility of life had driven him to nihilism; however, upon further meditation, he concluded that even a life with very little is to be desired over death. A scrawny, begging dog is better than a dead lion, even with its royal mane, intimidating teeth, and impressive musculature. What makes the difference? Hope. How poetic! Hope is the hope. For the dead, there is no option of hope. The story is written. The book is closed. There is no chance of improvement. Yet for the living, they can declare "Dum spiro, spero," "While I breathe - I hope." Yet, that is not all.

In Hebrews 9, the author also acknowledges the beauty in only having one life to live.

READ HEBREWS 9:27-28.

What do you observe about this passage?

_____

_____

_____

His acknowledgment of death's inevitability is followed immediately by the conviction that Jesus also lived once, and will return once again to bring salvation to those who are waiting for Him. This is good news for those who are waiting for Him, and it is further proof that there is value in our brief lives. As we live life to the fullest, we wait in hopeful anticipation that Jesus will return again to take His people home!

Isaiah preaches yet another perspective on life's meaning in Isaiah 38: "Only the living can thank [the Lord]" (v. 19). For the believer, there is not only value in life, but purpose as well. There is good work to be done, we dare not lay idle until Christ returns. Our purpose is to worship (thank) the Lord while we wait for His return, and do this to the best of our ability in every moment we are given. This is why life is meaningful. This is why being a begging dog is better than being a dead lion. In the midst of all the hunger and struggle, the begging dog is not confined by its past. The way things are may not be the way things will always be. We, the begging dogs, can bring glory to God and enjoy Him deeply as long as we live. After all, He is worthy of that glory.

When we live our lives for our own personal fame and gain, the end of life is a dreadful thought. The window of opportunity to advance our personal kingdoms closes when life ends. Not only this, but the value of the wealth we have earned loses all value to us when we are gone. We cannot enjoy the fruits of our personal kingdom forever. The fruits are temporary and so are we. However, followers of Jesus know there is a kingdom that lasts beyond death that is currently under construction and can be enjoyed forever. This is the kingdom of heaven.

What kingdom are you tempted to build instead of God's kingdom?

_____

_____

_____

_____

_____

_____

_____

The wisest man who ever lived recognized that it is better to live with however little that we are given than to die with much because the little we are given can bless the Lord a lot. Isaiah reminded us that it is good to bless the Lord with our thanks and worship as long as we live. Take a moment to thank the Lord, in this moment, for involving us in His ministry and giving us, as the hymnist wrote, "strength for today and bright hope for tomorrow."

DAY FIFTY-THREE

SCRIPTURE READING
Luke 15:11-32

When the story of the prodigal son is told, we are often reminded
of the times when we have acted like the prodigal son.

READ LUKE 15:11-32.

What stands out to you about
the story when you read it?

Perhaps you had a rebellious teenage phase where you disregarded the loving counsel of your parents. Maybe you needed the Gospel to be shared with you numerous times before you finally understood Jesus' offer. At the very least, you can remember sins you have committed that you had to bring before the Lord humbly, asking Him to forgive you and remind you of His love.

Everyone can relate to the son who ran away. We have all squandered the graces of our Savior and worshiped lifeless idols instead of the true God. We all need to return to the Father day after day in confession, and when we do, He always takes us in with open arms. Praise the Lord!

What about the older brother? He despised the celebration of his restored younger brother. He was more concerned with being adequately recognized and compensated for his labor and loyalty than celebrating his family being whole again. He desired to be superior to his brother and feared that he would be overlooked and under-appreciated. In his heart, it seems he was so concerned with his reputation and to-do list that he forgot to enjoy his father's blessings. If we look carefully, we may find that we are more like the older brother than we think. We may need to hear God say again, "Everything I have is yours" (Lk. 15:31).

When was a time that you were so distracted by your concerns that you missed out on enjoying the blessings God has given you?

_____

_____

_____

_____

Most of us in America live our lives at break-neck speeds. There is so much to do, so many opportunities to take, so much money to earn, and so many luxuries to enjoy. Often, we are addicted to saying yes to more, and we are immersed in a culture that celebrates those who do. The individual who works eighty hours a week to turn his or her small business into a corporate giant is praised with no thought given to the spouse and family who may feel abandoned. The one who lives a balanced life of worship, work, rest, marriage, family, and friends is often overlooked and deemed ordinary and uneventful. Yet, Jesus calls us to live for His pleasure above all others.

When was the last time you counted your blessings?
Recount a few right now and right them down.

_____

_____

_____

We will miss a mountain of blessings that God has for us today if we fixate on tomorrow. You have the freedom to "eat your bread with pleasure, and drink your wine with a cheerful heart" (Ecc. 9:7). You may be tempted to read this with hesitation. Choosing to relish God's abundant goodness to us can feel awkward or wrong. I'd like to propose that even though worldly hedonism is definitively anti-Christian, Christian hedonism, or seeking our highest pleasure in Jesus, is definitively God-glorifying! As John Piper commonly says,: "God is most glorified in us when we are most satisfied in him." Enjoying his blessings can, and should, be enjoyed as an act of worship to God! We must fight our older brother tendencies to be consumed with earning, and eat our bread *with pleasure*!

> What blessings can you thank the Lord for? What can
> you ask Him for assistance in worshipfully enjoying?

_____

_____

_____

_____

_____

_____

_____

_____

_____

_____

Life is short and unpredictable. It is "like vapor that appears for a little while, then vanishes" (Jam. 4:14). Death arrives for the strong and the weak alike, but God desires us to delight ourselves in Him and worship Him with every moment and blessing we are given. "Take delight in the Lord, and he will give you your heart's desires" (Ps. 37:4). Let us not overlook the blessings we are surrounded by as members of God's family.

DAY FIFTY-FOUR

SCRIPTURE READING
Psalm 128:1-6

What a blessing it is for a need to be met when it appears. Hopefully, you have experienced this at least once. Imagine sitting in line at your favorite fast-food drive-thru. You decide to splurge and order your favorite meal and an extra large order of fries; and when you get to the window, the cashier tells you that the person in front of you already paid for it. A delightfully unexpected gift right when you thought you had to pay the price.

It is nice to be surprised by a need met before it becomes a burden, but now imagine how differently it would feel to have a need met after months of trying to meet it yourself. For some, this may look like a compilation of bills. Every month, you may have to scrape together every last penny to pay the mortgage, car lease, student loan, or medical bill statements. The savings have run out, the interest is piling up, and the job is requiring more overtime hours to make ends meet. If a mysterious, generous donor were to pay off your student loan all at once, this would be life-changing! An immediate, full relief from a heavy, nagging burden.

> What was one of your most significant needs
> that was met outside of your expectations?

_____

_____

_____

Think back to your life before you started following Christ. Our sin was far too great a price to pay, and it had tainted everything good that God had created. But God sent Jesus to pay the price for us. It was Jesus himself who said, "Come to me, all of you who are weary and burdened, and I will give you rest" (Matt. 11:28). What kind of rest is He talking about? Rest from the tireless, worthless labor of trying to earn God's favor. We can rest because Jesus' work alone is sufficient to earn God's favor. He now stands in our place, so that when the Father looks at us, He sees Jesus' righteousness. There is nothing left to earn and nothing to prove for those in Christ! So, when we read Solomon's declaration that "God has already accepted [our] works," we can have even more confidence that God has accepted us because Jesus made sure of it (Ecc. 9:7)!

A natural reaction to such a glorious truth is to celebrate! How could we not? We were dead, now we live. We were blind, now we see.

The celebration magnifies our joyful experience. Josh Garrells wrote a beautiful illustration of how our salvation response looks:

> "Skipping like a calf loosed from its stall
> I'm free to love once and for all
> And even when I fall I'll get back up
> For the joy that overflows my cup"

Have you ever had joy overflow into a celebration? If so, write down why the celebration increased the joy. If not, take a moment to imagine such a situation. Consider how a wedding, graduation, or anniversary celebration increases the joy of the occasion.

_____

_____

_____

_____

READ PSALM 128.

What do you notice about this passage?

_____

_____

_____

Solomon and the Psalmist agree—there is much to celebrate in life, especially in the fact that we are loved by God, our maker, creator, and sustainer. You are cherished and highly favored by the God of the universe! And, as a result, you can read Psalm 128 with excitement. You will "be happy and it will go well for you" (Ps. 128:2). "The man who fears the Lord will be blessed" (Ps. 128:4). Of course, this is not to be interpreted as us getting whatever we want and when we want it; but, we can be sure that there is sweetness and blessing in this life (and the next) for those who fear the Lord.

Followers of Jesus have more invincible joys to celebrate than anyone else on earth. Enjoy your life because you have a sure hope! Enjoy your blessings because your Father loves to bless His children! Enjoy your freedom, because you are fully known and loved! "Sing to the Lord, you his faithful ones, and praise his holy name. For his anger lasts only a moment, but his favor, a lifetime. Weeping may stay overnight, but there is joy in the morning" (Ps. 30:4-5).

Take a moment to to start your day with a prayer of
gratitude to God for the blessings you have in this life.

_____

_____

_____

_____

_____

_____

_____

DAY FIFTY-FIVE

SCRIPTURE READING
Colossians 3:12-17

Ask a farmer what the most rewarding season of the year is, and she will most likely answer "harvest." Months of toil finally result in bountiful reaping. Monotonous, anxious waiting is replaced by fruitful closure. The farmer feels a deep sense of relief and accomplishment as she looks out over their fields. A job well done. It is enough food to last the year. Now what? Does the farmer just leave the crops in the ground until the family is ready to eat? The produce will only stay fresh for so long in the ground before spoiling. Without being harvested, processed, and properly stored, the bounty will be missed. Harvest is a time to rejoice, but it is also a time to act urgently. It is time to get to work!

A farmer's harvest is a beautiful picture of what we are called to in life as followers of Jesus. We have peace before God because of Christ's finished work on the cross. Jesus perfectly sowed the seeds of salvation that we could never sow, to provide a harvest of life and freedom that we could never grow. This is incomprehensibly good news. After thousands of years of waiting for the promised Messiah, deliverance has come! Jesus provided everything necessary for life in godliness. And His last words on earth told us how we should live.

> "Go, therefore, and make disciples of all nations, baptizing them in the name of the Father and of the Son and of the Holy Spirit, teaching them to observe everything I have commanded you. And remember, I am with you always, to the end of the age" (Matt. 28:19-20)

Jesus' final words were a mission. He calls His people to action until He returns. The Gospel harvest has begun, and there is much work to do.

> When was a time that a task was made easier
> by what you knew was at the finish line?

_____

_____

_____

Solomon knew that there was no more work to do once life ended. He felt urgency because he understood that life was short and unpredictable. Though we have a different mission ("Go, therefore, and make disciples..."), our urgency is the same. Jesus is going to return for us, and before He does, He "wants everyone to be saved and to come to the knowledge of the truth" (1 Tim. 2:4). How, then, should we live? Let us look at the apostle Paul's words.

In Colossians, Paul implores the church to worship. Read Colossians 3:12-17. What instructions does Paul give in these verses?

_____

_____

_____

_____

Paul understood the pressure the church was facing. He, of all people, understood the unpredictability of life. At the time of writing this letter, Paul was in prison for preaching the message of Jesus, but this did not deter him from continuing to teach the way of life.

Paul's counsel in Chapter 3 can be summarized in four characteristics: forgiveness, love, peace, and wisdom. They are definitive Christian traits because they were defining traits of Jesus. We are to forgive as Jesus forgave, love as He loved, pursue peace as Jesus pursued peace, and understand the word of God as Jesus did. When all that remains of the Christian is their legacy remembered by those they loved, these characteristics should be what are remembered. In case that list was not comprehensive enough, Paul concludes his thought with an overarching principle: "...whatever you do, in word or in deed, do everything in the name of the Lord Jesus..." (Col. 3:17). The Gospel of Jesus should be the motivation for and the guiding principle of our brief ministry on this earth.

What is one characteristic of Jesus that you can ask the
Holy Spirit to help cultivate in you?

_____

_____

_____

_____

_____

_____

_____

_____

_____

_____

_____

_____

_____

Harvest is a time to rejoice, but it is also a time to act urgently. No matter the hardships or trials we may face, we get to enjoy the freedom of Jesus and advance God's kingdom. Let us press on in life with forgiveness, love, peace, and wisdom to spread the good news of Jesus!

WEEK
12

Steward

ECCLESIASTES 11

"SEND YOUR BREAD
ON THE SURFACE OF
THE WATER, FOR
AFTER MANY DAYS
YOU MAY FIND IT."

ECCLESIASTES 11:1

"WE LEARN FROM
OUR GARDENS TO DEAL
WITH THE MOST URGENT
QUESTION OF OUR
TIME: HOW MUCH
IS ENOUGH?"

WENDELL BERRY

DAY FIFTY-SIX

SCRIPTURE READING
Job 38-41

Now that you are making your way to the end of this book, it's time to try something a little different.[13] We've been reading small bite-sized chunks of Scripture each day, but you've got four chapters to consider this morning. You can do it—I promise! While you might get a sense of the overall scope of this passage by reading a small portion, the real punch of the text is to consider it all as one unit.

A little context before you get started. We are reading the book of Job, which is the story of one man's life of suffering. Satan has crushed Job and all that he has, and all that he loves has been taken away. The story of this suffering is told in the opening chapter, and the bulk of the book is Job wrestling with God about why horri-

[13] This week's reflections are written by Matt Rogers, one of the pastors of Christ Fellowship Cherrydale in Greenville, South Carolina.

ble things like what he's experiencing. As he grapples with these ideas, Job's friends attempt to provide answers and direction for him. Most of their supposed wisdom and help is actually terrible. It's a jumbled mess of bad theology and weak answers. Neither Job nor his friends seem able to answer the questions that suffering demands. It seems that the book will end without an answer.

But then God speaks. He's been silent throughout the book, merely allowing Job's friends to provide their attempts at understanding the suffering Job is experiencing. Now it's God's turn to answer. But His answer isn't what you might expect.

READ JOB CHAPTERS 38-41.

Write down the main theme of these chapters in the space below.

_____

_____

_____

These chapters point to God's omniscience and omnipotence. Omniscience means that God knows everything, and omnipotence means that God can do anything. He has all knowledge and all power.

People simply don't possess all knowledge and power. This reality haunts us, particularly when we go through hard things. Our suffering exposes the fact that we lack the power to stop pain from entering our lives, and we lack the knowledge to understand why that suffering is there in the first place. We want to know the purpose for our suffering, but we don't have the ability to see it from God's perspective. Our humanity frustrates us. We know it is true, but we don't like the words that Solomon writes in Ecclesiastes 11: "you don't know the work of God who makes everything" (v. 5).

You can either kick against this reality, or you can embrace it. Much like the toddler trying to kick free of his dad's arms, though, all of our temper tantrums will not give us the knowledge or power that we lack. We are called to simply embrace the reality that we are limited, finite people. This fact should humble us. There's much about the world, about God, and about His purposes in the world that we will never know. And that's ok.

These facts do not mean that it's always wrong to ask questions when we go through hard times. God isn't immune to our suffering. After all, Jesus Himself suffered mightily on this earth and was willing to entrust Himself to God's good purposes even though the path ahead seemed overwhelming (Lk. 22:42). It's this same level of trust that is required for God's people on this earth. We are to be people who willingly say "not my will, but yours." While this may seem like a daunting task, it's actually reassuring to simply entrust yourself to someone with all power and knowledge.

We never fully experience this type of trust in this life, but perhaps the idea of flying will get us close. When you step onto a plane, most of us are entering a world where we lack power and knowledge. From the vantage of the cheap seats, most have no clue how a plane flies, what all of those buttons do, how to navigate the runway and takeoff, or how to control the plane in the air so that it follows the prescribed flight path. Not only don't we know how to do these things, but we also aren't in the pilot's position. We aren't the ones flying the plane. And unless you've flown a different airline than I have, they don't make planes with little joysticks attached to row 57, seat B, that allow you to override the pilot's intentions and redirect the plane. We simply sit back, eat the dainty delicacies the stewardess provides, and watch an average movie on an all-too-small screen.

This illustration points us in the right direction in understanding the trust that we should give our God. While our lives aren't meant to be consumed with snacking and binge watching shows, we are passive when it comes to running the universe. That's God's job. Ours is to take a deep breath and trust Him to do what He alone can do. When we go through rough air we don't panic because we know that our captain knows what He's doing. When He speaks to us through His word, we listen because we know that He's telling us something important. And, when we arrive safely at our heavenly destination, we praise Him for getting us where we needed to be even when we did not know what all He was doing.

Where do you need to trust God today?

_____

_____

_____

_____

_____

_____

_____

_____

DAY FIFTY-SEVEN

SCRIPTURE READING
Matthew 13:1-9

There's nothing overtly mentioned about the work in the book of Ecclesiastes. However, the book is filled with implications for our evangelistic efforts. For example, if all of life is futile and money and power and fame will not satisfy the human heart, then we have a good opportunity to hold out the hope of the gospel to those who seek after these worldly trinkets and come up short. We can present a better hope for a better world made possible through the finished work of Jesus Christ.

Not only that, but there are allusions to the work of evangelism in passages like Ecclesiastes 11:6, which reads: "In the morning sow your seed, and at evening do not let your hand rest, because you don't know which will succeed."

READ MATTHEW 13:1-9.

What connection do you notice between
Ecclesiastes 11 and Matthew 13?

_____

_____

_____

_____

_____

The sower in Jesus' parable scatters seeds of the gospel on differing soils. Some do nothing, others produce lasting fruit. The problem is that the sower doesn't know what kind of soil he is scattering the seed in. Only in time does it become clear. If we simply break the 4 soils into quarters, then the text suggests that there's only a 25% return on investment. 75% of the seed is wasted on soils (or people) that do not produce lasting fruit. If the sower had all knowledge, then he could simply choose to invest all of the gospel seed in the good soil. But he doesn't. So he must continue to indiscriminately scatter the seed of the gospel and trust that God will allow some of it to produce a harvest.

The parachurch organization Cru has a compelling definition of evangelism that captures this idea. They say that evangelism is "taking the initiative to share the gospel in the power of the Holy Spirit and leaving the results to God." Notice the role of the person in this definition:

→ They take initiative

→ The share the gospel

Then notice God's role:

➔ He gives the power

➔ He produces the results

This perspective provides freedom for the work of evangelism. We don't have to have the power, nor do we have the obligation to produce the results. That's all God's to do. But we do have to scatter the seed of the gospel, and we do have to share that gospel clearly and compellingly.

We can be prone to do a bit of mental arithmetic in our minds before we share the gospel. One person looks or acts like the kind of person who might respond favorably, or at least might not condemn us for sharing, so we take the risk to engage in conversion. Another person seems hostile to the gospel or has a background that would suggest that he or she isn't the least bit interested in hearing about Jesus. So we don't share.

Matthew 13 and Ecclesiastes 11 call Christians to resist this temptation. We don't know what will succeed. Since it is God who produces the fruit, since it is He who brings about conversion, we should scatter the seed of the gospel indiscriminately to any and all who might listen. We shouldn't judge their readiness or willingness to receive the truth of the gospel based on our wisdom or instincts. It is ours to share. It is God's to produce fruit.

This leads us back to the two areas that you and I are responsible for. First, we must know how to share the gospel. This doesn't mean that we must master the gospel, for who can plumb the depths of the realities of God's saving work? But it does mean that we should know the basic message of how God acted to save sinners through Jesus Christ. Paul provides a summary of the gospel message in 1 Corinthians 15: "For I passed on to you as most important what I also received: that

Christ died for our sins according to the Scriptures, that he was buried, that he was raised on the third day according to the Scriptures" (v. 3-4). In other words, the gospel is the message of Jesus Christ. It's not a list of doctrinal facts that you must memorize, but truth about who Jesus is, what He came to do, why He was necessary, and how someone can and should respond to Jesus' invitation of salvation.

Next, you must take initiative. For most of us, this is the key factor that we lack. We have enough knowledge of the Bible and of the gospel to share, but we often don't share because we allow fears and insecurities and busyness to sidetrack us. Maybe we've been on the receiving end of evangelism gone bad, and we don't want to turn someone off by coming across too strongly. Or maybe we fear that we won't know what to say if the person asks questions. Or perhaps we have hidden sin in our life that causes us to avoid sharing for fear that our hypocrisy will be exposed. Whatever the reason we are tempted to shy away from evangelism, God presses us to trust Him enough to overcome our fears and take initiative anyway. If you wait for a time when you aren't afraid or when all of the variables line up perfectly, then you will simply never share the gospel. You may not have the power to change another person's heart, but you do have the power to take initiative for your own obedience to Christ's command to share and then trust Him to allow some of the seed that you sow to produce a harvest.

Where do you need to take initiative to share the good news today?

_____

_____

_____

_____

DAY FIFTY-EIGHT

SCRIPTURE READING
Philippians 4:2-9

Rejoice is an odd word if you stop to think about it. The root word "joy" gets a bit lost with the adjusted spelling. It's better to think of the word as a combination of the root "joy" and the prefix "re." So literally to rejoice is to experience joy again. It's the act of multiplying joy over and over again. What a great thought! Wouldn't it be nice to experience joy on repeat in your life?

READ PHILIPPIANS 4:4-9

and notice what Paul says about rejoicing in this passage.

_____

_____

_____

You get a sense of the counterintuitive nature of rejoicing by the fact that Paul has to tell the people to rejoice twice. He repeats his command to rejoice, and the second time it's said with exclamatory emphasis. Rejoice! Notice back in verses 2 and 3 that this command comes after Paul addresses relational discord in the church. This might be something that would cause us to grow discouraged rather than rejoice. But he reminds us that we should rejoice in the fact that our eternal destiny is secure. In other words, even though there are relational challenges in this world, Christians should not lose sight of the fact that there is a future hope for restoration in the world to come.

So rejoice! The rejoicing that Paul commends is "in the Lord." In other words, don't rejoice in your circumstances, or else you will find plenty to drag you down. You can rejoice in the Lord, however. If you think about Him—His goodness, His love, His eternal care for you—then there is an ever-present source of joy regardless of what circumstances you are walking through. In this way, every day can foster renewed joy, or rejoicing. When is the last time you remember feeling overwhelmed with a sense of joy in the Lord?

_____

_____

_____

Many of us might struggle to answer this question. Often we find ourselves so wrapped up in the circumstances of our lives that we find it hard to step back and bask in the joy that is found in knowing and being loved by God.

Marriage or parenting can provide an illustration of this reality. There's plenty of joy to go around on the wedding day or the birthday of a new child. It's a joyous occasion to say the least. But fast forward a few decades, and many times the joy fades into a plethora of details, tasks, frustrations, calendars, and budgets. Couples often become co-workers who partner together in an effort to make their way through life's challenges. In all of that activity, it's possible to lose sight of the joy we once found in the relationship. The same is true in parenting. Dirty diapers, snotty noses, discipline issues, schooling, bad attitudes, and the like all make for busy and frustrated parents. Multiply this over a few years, and a parent might find that the joy they once found in their relationship with a son or daughter has now grown cold.

Thankfully, God gives us glimpses of this first love from time to time. Maybe it's a date night where you get to step back and just enjoy being together without something else to do. Or it could be a picture that pops up on your phone of a cute little kid that reminds you of the joy and privilege it is to be a parent.

God often does the same for us when it comes to our relationship with Him. It might be in a church worship service or during a long hike in the woods or through a conversation with a friend or through reading the word and praying. He breaks into the rhythms of our lives and reminds us of His love for us and our eternal destiny. He tenderly calls us to rest in our relationship with Him and find joy in the fact that we can call Him our Heavenly Father.

Paul encourages Christians to strive to live in this place. We are called to rejoice daily in His love. This is true for Christians, and it's true for churches as a whole. We must strive, together, to call one another to find joy in the Lord. It seems that the church in Ephesus lost this joy because John reproves them in Revelation and writes: "But I have this against you: you have abandoned the love you had at first" (Rev. 2:4). Apparently, the church's love for the Lord had waned. They'd lost the joy in knowing and loving God.

May the same not be said of us. The only way for churches as a whole to protect their affection and joy in the Lord is for the individual Christians who make up those churches to do just that. Each of us must put ourselves in the place to be reminded of the joy that comes from God each day. We have to fight the drift of busyness and complacency. We have to resist the urge toward outward religious performance that lacks a genuine heart of love for God. We must strive to stoke the fires of our joy for the Lord on a regular basis.

And, we should encourage others in this direction as well. We should speak the word of God to others in our church so that they are reminded of the beauty of God's love. When we see others just going through the motions or stuck in places of sin and apathy, we should kindly and winsomely call them to joy in the Lord. When we gather with the church on Sundays, we should make it our aim to speak words of joy to those around us so that we add fuel to the smoldering fire of joy that they may be experiencing at that moment.

How is God producing joy in your life?

_____

_____

_____

DAY FIFTY-NINE

SCRIPTURE READING
Isaiah 40:28-31

Wouldn't it be nice to never get tired? We all have a limited store-house of energy to get us through the day, and many days we are simply exhausted by the time we get to our bed at night. The compounding impact of busy days means that many of us never seem to catch up on sleep, so we move into each new day with depleted energy. This is true for young adults, and it's even more true the older you get. We are all limited people in so many ways.

READ ISAIAH 40:28-31.

What does this passage tell us about God?

What does this passage say God will do for us?

In verse 28, Isaiah points out that God doesn't get tired or weary. Right before this, He's just said that God made all things. He's the Creator of Heaven and Earth, but He doesn't get tired. Maybe you've tried to create something—whether it's a term paper for school, an art project, or simply a new arrangement of your household furniture or a new color of paint. When we create something, our energy is spent. Our battery drains from the expenditure needed to create. But not God. He can speak all things into existence and not get tired doing it.

Psalm 121 makes the same point:

> I lift my eyes toward the mountains.
> Where will my help come from?
> My help comes from the Lord,
> the Maker of heaven and earth.
> He will not allow your foot to slip;
> your Protector will not slumber.
> Indeed, the Protector of Israel
> does not slumber or sleep (v. 1-4).

God has a surplus of energy. He never runs out. It's His in an overflowing measure. So He is uniquely able to give it to others who have needs. This is where Isaiah goes next. The faint and the powerless need strength, and God is able and willing to give them that strength from His vast supply. He notes that even young people get tired and weary, so all people, young and old alike, will need to find strength from God.

God gives strength to anyone who "trusts in the Lord" (v. 31). Trust is the means by which frail and tired people get access to God's strength. They depend on Him for help, rather than relying on their strength alone. They tap into the strength that God has and wants to give to others.

Those who trust in the Lord are promised renewed strength (v. 31). This is good news because people don't have the ability to renew their strength on their own. While we might be able to get a good night's sleep and feel refreshed in the morning, sleep is not sufficient to renew our hearts and our souls. We grow weary in more ways than just the fact that we lack physical strength. We also lack the strength needed to find joy, hope, and peace in our hearts. We run out of the will to love and serve others and do good in the world around us. We get discouraged by the brokenness that we see in our lives, in the lives of others, and in the world around us. God can renew the strength of our heart and soul.

The outcome of this renewal is that we soar, run, and walk without giving up. It's an all-encompassing type of renewal. The image is of a bird of prey majestically flying over the water or a cheetah sprinting across the field. You watch these animals in action, and it seems like they will never run out of energy. God renews the heart of His people so they can soar!

Notice in verse 28 that God does not faint; so, in verse 31, we will not faint either. Our power comes from His power. In the New Testament, this power source is the Holy Spirit. He is given to believers to power them through life's mission. He is the source of strength and the way that God renews the hearts of His people. We seek to be filled with His Spirit so that we can be renewed to soar, run, and walk through life (Eph. 5:18).

How have you seen God renew your Spirit?

_____

_____

_____

_____

_____

_____

_____

_____

_____

_____

_____

_____

_____

DAY SIXTY

SCRIPTURE READING
1 Timothy 4:11-16

If you compiled all of the youth group t-shirts ever made in the history of youth groups and ran the numbers, I'd imagine that there's one Bible verse that would show up more than any other.

READ 1 TIMOTHY 4:11-16.

**Why is this verse such a classic
verse to quote to teenagers?**

_____

_____

_____

It's true that Timothy was a young pastor, likely in his 20s. He'd had studied under Paul and was now leading a church. This role almost certainly had him leading people who were much older than himself. Paul exhorts him to not let his age hinder his work in God's mission.

This is a natural connection to the end of Ecclesiastes 11. First, in verse 9 we read "rejoice, young person, while you are young and let your heart be glad in the days of your youth." Then, in verse 10 Solomon writes, "remove sorrow from your heart, and put away pain from your flesh, because youth and the prime of life are fleeting." So Solomon's counsel, based on the fleeting nature of life, is to fully embrace the season of life that you are in. And, particularly for those who are young, they should passionately pursue life during this season because the days of youth are short-lived. You won't be young, forever, after all!

The question for the young is, "What does it mean to live life fully when I'm young?" After all, this is what all young people are trying to do. They want to live the life, they just define the ideal life differently. Is the ideal life one of hedonism? Is it drunkenness? Sexual sin? Permiscuiness? Lazy days doing a bunch of nothing? Paul says, No! The life for the young is to "set an example for the believers in speech, in conduct, in love, in faith, and in purity" (1 Tim 4:12). It's to "give your attention to the public reading, exhortation, and teaching" (1 Tim 4:13). The young should use their days of health and energy and vitality to lead the way in godly living and devotion to God's word. They may not have the wisdom of older saints, but the young can run hard after God and His mission in the world.

Assuming that you are older than 25, think back to the decade between when you were 15 and 25. How did you spend those years? When you look back on that decade do you think that you stewarded the time in meaningful ways? Do you have any regrets?

If you are like most of us, you have plenty of regrets. We don't need to overstate the argument here. Of course, there's a natural process of maturation and development that is at work at this time that makes us all a bit crazy. And we are living in a messed up world that throws things at us that we are not ready for. But that shouldn't obscure the fact that God gave us those years, and He expects us to honor Him with the lives we live during our teens and 20s.

And think about the huge potential for people in their youth. As a whole, they are healthy and able to engage in work without growing tired like older people. They've got developing minds that are capable of learning the truth about God and His work in the world. They are incredibly flexible so they can jump and move quickly and without the challenges that come from a family that has been rooted in a community for a long time. They are making decisions about who they might date or marry, so they have the potential to partner with another person for God's mission. Some may not marry, so they have the capacity to live with flexibility that's not possible for those with a spouse or children. Many are earning money in this season and are determining how they will use those resources—either to create an easy life or to aid God's work around the world. The list could go on and on.

There's another opportunity for youth, and it's one that's inherent to Paul's instructions in chapter 4. He says that others are looking at their example. The fact that youth is a season of life known for craziness means that those who pursue God and His purposes during this stage will stand out even more. They will be positioned to testify to why they've determined that living according to God's design and plan is the best way to live.

There's one final point of encouragement for the not-so-young, which is many of us reading this book. Paul encourages Titus to build a church where older men are teaching younger men and older women are teaching younger women (Titus 2:1-8). While you may not be able to relive your youth, you can invest your life in others so that they avoid some of the mistakes you made and choose to love and obey God instead. Don't sulk in regret at the youth that has passed you by, but choose to use the wisdom of your age to help other youth run well.

> How is God calling you to use this
> season of your life for His glory?

_____

_____

_____

_____

_____

_____

_____

WEEK
13

Remember

ECCLESIASTES 12

"SO REMEMBER YOUR
CREATOR IN THE DAYS OF
YOUR YOUTH: BEFORE THE
DAYS OF ADVERSITY COME,
AND THE YEARS APPROACH
WHEN YOU WILL SAY,
'I HAVE NO DELIGHT
IN THEM'"

ECCLESIASTES 7:11-12

"OLD AGE IS LIKE
EVERYTHING ELSE. TO
MAKE A SUCCESS OF
IT, YOU'VE GOT TO
START YOUNG."

THEODORE
ROOSEVELT

DAY SIXTY-ONE

SCRIPTURE READING

Job 13:13-28

Ever had a bad day? How about a bad month? Or even a year? Sometimes it might seem like you've just had a downright bad life, right?[14]

There's no minimizing how difficult our lives can be. Through the years as a pastor of a local church, I've heard some terrible stories. Some people have suffered for foolish things they've done. Others have been crippled by sin that was committed against them. Many have experienced unspeakable loss and trauma that paralyzed them then and still grips them today.

Today's reading comes from the middle of the book of Job. If anyone can relate to suffering, it's Job. His story is told in the Wisdom books of the Old Testament, and we've considered this story

[14] This week's reflections are written by Matt Rogers, one of the pastors of Christ Fellowship Cherrydale in Greenville, South Carolina.

in other weeks already. Right in the middle, as Job's friends give him all sorts of terrible counsel, Job speaks.

READ JOB 13:13-28.

What do you notice about these verses?

_____

_____

_____

_____

It's a pretty strong statement to say, "Even if he kills me, I will hope in Him" (v. 15). This doesn't mean that Job is overjoyed at the pain he's experienced. He's certainly not. Like Solomon writes in Ecclesiastes 12, when the days of adversity come, we will say, "I have no delight in them" (v. 1). We are right to lament the difficulty we experience, but Job models a persevering hope in the Lord amid the pain.

Job's hope isn't found in changing circumstances but "in the Lord." This is a common refrain in these books. For example, Psalm 20:7-8 says "Some take pride in chariots, and others in horses, but we take pride in the name of the Lord our God. They collapse and fall, but we rise and stand firm." Other translations render this "we trust in the name of the Lord our God." Others trust in military might, but the Psalmist places his hope in the Lord.

This is an appropriate picture of our suffering. The world around us is like an enemy army coming to attack and kill us. Our hope isn't based on the fact that we have the power to defend ourselves. Our hope is in the Lord. If He is for us, we have nothing to fear (Rom. 8:37).

The book of Ecclesiastes comes to a close with a reminder to trust in the Lord. The reminder isn't as overt as it is in other books, but Solomon is clear that adversity is coming. Though the years of one's youth are hopeful, those days are fleeting and soon comes the reality of old age and death. We may know that death is a reality, but when we are young, it's far easier to press this reality out of our minds. But with each passing year, the shadow of the valley of death grows.

Solomon doesn't want this reality to take us off guard. He wants to prepare others for the fact that for all of the wealth and power and women and wisdom he had, he was still not able to do anything to keep death at bay. And he couldn't keep suffering or evil away either. Even before he would die, days of adversity would come.

What do you do when days of adversity come to you? Do you give up? Do you get overwhelmed? Do you forget the promises of God? We've all been there, so don't take those questions as accusations. We know the difficulty of placing our hope in the Lord when inevitable adversity takes hold of our lives.

Let's let Solomon's wisdom, Job's example, and our past failures spur us on to a different path in the future. The key to suffering well is to hope in the Lord. It's to remind ourselves early and often of the hope we have through Jesus Christ. You may have heard someone talk about "speaking the gospel to yourself," and this is often what they are referring to by this notion. The idea is that you talk to yourself more than anyone else in the world. Every day, you are narrating your own life to yourself. You are telling yourself things about God, about His work in the world, about how to interpret your circumstances. We all need to grow in our ability to speak good news to ourselves in those moments. We don't have to wait for a preacher or podcast to remind us to hope in God. We can train ourselves to go to His word and to spend time in prayer. We can rest in the promises He's made for His people in His word. When we do, we learn to hope in God, and God, in His grace, gives us the perseverance necessary to respond well when the days of adversity come.

How is God giving you hope?

_____

_____

_____

_____

_____

_____

_____

_____

_____

_____

_____

_____

_____

_____

_____

DAY SIXTY-TWO

SCRIPTURE READING
John 14:1-7

If you've ever had to pick out a casket, then you know how terrible that shopping experience is. They try to lessen the awkwardness of the moment with the displays of various caskets for you to check out. There are various styles and models, each made of different materials and shaped in different ways. As you browse, you know that you are picking out the resting place for the body of someone whom you loved deeply and who is now gone forever. It's a miserable experience.

Ecclesiastes 12 is all about death. The verses describe the scene of another life that's come to an end. As the mourners walk around in the street, Solomon says, "a mere mortal is headed to his eternal home" (v. 5). On the surface, this sounds like a terrible reality. Another casket with another body and another eternal death.

But Christians have an eternal home that is far superior to this life.

READ JOHN 14:1-7.

What does this verse say about our eternal home?

_____

_____

_____

_____

_____

The eternal home of a Christian is a place of joy, not dread. While death is horrible, we do not need to despair when a believer goes to his or her eternal home. It's astounding to consider this reality because, in essence, a casket is a fitting resting place for humans. Even the greatest among us are sinful and broken. When we die, our bodies are frail or broken. The beauty of youth is gone. Many enter death tired and weary. You might expect that the resting place for such brokenness would be a lowly box akin to a lowly park bench that houses a homeless man for the night.

But God vastly upgrades our dwelling place after death. We do not get what our lives deserve; rather, we receive what Christ has earned. All that is His is now ours, and that includes His eternal home. We are told in John 14 that Jesus has been working on this heavenly dwelling since the time He left this earth. He's a carpenter by trade, so you have to imagine that He knows what He's done. And, since He was active in the world's creation in the first place (Col. 1:16), we must imagine that this eternal home that He's been working on is going to far eclipse anything we've seen on this earth.

We tend to imagine this house like a mansion sitting on a hill overlooking a lake. But in this part of the world, the idea would likely refer to a single house with rooms added on for additional family members. Many homes had unfinished roofs, so when a son or daughter married and new people were added to the family, they could just build additional rooms upstairs in the family house. This way those with little resources could take advantage of living in the home that their parents or grandparents had established. Also, due to the communal nature of the culture, the more family you had living in one place the better.

This is a really beautiful picture of our eternal home. God is building a house and he's building it for those new people who are being added to the family through faith in Jesus Christ. As they become a part of His family, He adds additional rooms to the house where they will live forever in community with God's people.

The heavenly home is a far cry from the lowly casket. Mere mortals don't dwell in a heavenly home unless God makes that possible. He promises to do just that for those who have faith in His Son. As a result, we who have that faith can have hope when we see the dwelling place of mortals in death. We know that we can't trust what our eyes can see. Yes, the body is resting in a casket, but the soul is present with the Lord in a place of eternal joy.

This fact should soften the experience of death and grief. It will not make the loss go away. Death still has quite a sting to it in our experience. But the Apostle Paul reminds us that this sting doesn't have the last word: "Death has been swallowed up in victory. Where, death, is your victory? Where, death, is your sting? The sting of sin is death, and the power of sin is the law. But thanks be to God, who gives us the victory through our Lord Jesus Christ" (1 Cor 15:54-57). Jesus has removed the sting of death, and one of the ways we should celebrate this reality is by focusing on the heavenly home that awaits.

Which brings us to a key question: How much do you think about heaven? For most of us, we tend to think about heaven more when we are going through suffering or when we know that death is approaching. But what if thoughts of heaven were the soundtrack of your life? The more you look forward to your heavenly home, the more you'll be prepared to endure and thrive in this life, especially as you get older and the difficulty of life increases.

How much do you think about heaven?
What could you do to think about heaven more?

DAY SIXTY-THREE

SCRIPTURE READING
1 Thessalonians 4:13-18

Let's imagine that you had 30 seconds to say the most encouraging thing possible to someone who was going through something hard. What would you say? Many times we feel like Job's friends as we try to give counsel and care to those who are hurting. Often, the best thing is just to be near the person, pray with them, and listen.

But there's also a time and a place for words. Our words can bring comfort and encouragement to those who are in a bad place, which is just where the Thessalonian church was. Persecution was normal for Christians at that time. Sin and suffering were everywhere. And, to make matters worse, many in the church assumed that Jesus would return soon. Now, as some Christians were dying and Jesus had not returned, the early Christians were nervous. What was happening? Had God forgotten about His promises?

READ 1 THESSALONIANS 4:13-18.

How does Paul encourage them?

_____

_____

_____

_____

_____

Here "fallen asleep" is a reference to death. Some in the church died, and Paul comforted the living Chrisitans by reminding them of what would happen to both Christians who died and to those who were alive when Jesus returned. What he shares is far more than Solomon knew in his day when he wrote that "the spirit returns to God who gave it" when a person dies (Ecc. 12:7).

The most important feature of Paul's explanation is the repeated idea that those who die will be with the Lord. They will meet the Lord in the air, and they will be with Him forever. In this way, the Spirit will fully return back to the God who gave it. But it will not just be the Spirit. Christians will not be disembodied beings floating around in heaven with just their souls. They will be raised like Jesus was raised, body and all. These new bodies will be without the impediments of sin and suffering, but they will be real bodies, seemingly much like the bodies that we have in this life, only better. Paul's encouragement to those suffering is that they will soon be with God, body and soul.

The same message should bring encouragement to us as well. We, too, live on this side of Jesus' life, death, and resurrection, and we await the return of the Lord Jesus Christ in the future. As we wait, we can easily lose heart in the suffering we experience and in the fact that so many have lived and died since Jesus walked on this earth. Like the Thessalonians, we can wonder if Jesus has forgotten us or if He is going to abandon His promises. Don't go there, Christian. Don't doubt the faithfulness of God. He's demonstrated His faithfulness through the pages of Scripture from cover to cover. He will surely see to it that He does exactly what He's promised to do.

Which means you will soon be with God!

We get a glimpse of this coming reality in this life from time to time. Think about a genuine time in your life when you felt especially close to God. Maybe it was in a quiet time early in the morning or in a church worship service. Maybe it was a late night walk or a quiet spot in the woods. There you experienced the reality that the nearness of God is your good (Ps. 73:28). You felt loved, accepted, safe. The bad thing about these experiences is that they are often short-lived in this life. We have to move back out into the real world and, at least in some sense, leave the sense of intimacy we were experiencing with God. Granted, we do not leave God's presence. He is always near to us through His Spirit, but our experience of His nearness does change. We get back to the hustle and bustle of our lives, and many times, we neglect intimacy with Him. Wouldn't it be nice if you could experience His nearness always?

This is the future hope for Christitians. When we die, we will awaken to a world where we will never not be near God. There will be nothing to stand in the way of experiencing His full love and joy. We will never be tempted to leave His side. We will never again get busy and forget about Him. We will be with Him forever.

This future hope should remind us of our present need for nearness and intimacy with God. If we are not experiencing a vibrant relationship with God, the issue isn't on His end. He's near to us through Christ and the presence of the Holy Spirit. He is never too busy or preoccupied to want to relate to us. His ear is always attentive and His arms always open to receive His children. So today, begin by asking God to give you a real sense of His love and care for you today. As James 4:8 reminds us: "Draw near to God, and He will draw near to you."

Are you enjoying the presence of God in your life right now? Why or why not?

_____

_____

_____

_____

_____

_____

_____

_____

_____

_____

DAY SIXTY-FOUR

SCRIPTURE READING
John 10:1-21

Solomon wrote the book of Ecclesiastes to provide guidance for his children and others who esteemed his wisdom. He wanted them to know the path to life and the path to ruin. The book ends (Ecclesiastes chapter 12) by saying that Solomon continued to teach and instruct others based on the wisdom given to Him by God. He compared his wise leadership to that of a Shepherd, who knows what is best for His sheep and leads them to places where they will thrive.

This isn't the first, and it will certainly not be the last, time that the image of a shepherd is used to describe God's leadership

READ JOHN 10:1-21.

What stands out to you about this passage?

_____

_____

_____

_____

Jesus says that He cares for people in the way a Shepherd cares for sheep. And the primary way that God leads His people is through His word. Notice the connection. Solomon leads people with the wisdom of his words, and Jesus leads people in the same way:

> The gatekeeper opens it for him, and the sheep hear *his voice*. He calls his own sheep by name and leads them out. When he has brought all his own outside, he goes ahead of them. The sheep follow him because they know *his voice* (Jn 10:3-4).

Sheep would learn the voice of their shepherd. Outside, these animals would hear all sorts of noises, and they'd pass by and hear other voices as well. But they'd know the voice of their shepherd. For one, they would be around this shepherd all of the time, so His voice would be common to them. Also, the shepherd would protect them from harm and lead them to places with ample food and water, so they would learn over time that it was in their best interest to listen to the shepherd's voice. They would want to do whatever that voice said.

Perhaps you've played a game that approximates this reality. You and a partner begin at the starting line. Ahead are all sorts of obstacles that you must avoid to make it safely across. The trick is that the person walking through the minefield is blindfolded, and his or her partner must lead them safely across while remaining back at the starting line. In other words, the blindfolded person is being directed simply by the other's words. Now, the game gets more complex if you play it with multiple teams trying to make it through at the same time. You might imagine how noisy it gets when 10 or 12 people are all trying to get their partner's attention as they move through the minefield. It often becomes a game of who can yell the loudest.

This is the picture Jesus paints in John 10. There are other voices vying for the attention of the sheep. Jesus says that these are coming to "steal and kill and destroy" (v. 10). These voices vie for our attention as well. The voices might be the sound of the broader culture attempting to redirect our attention away from Jesus. It might be the voice of persecution from those who seek to undermine our faith. The voices might be the lies of the Enemy who is seeking to twist God's truth and shipwreck our lives. Every day, we walk out into a minefield of voices yelling for our attention.

In contrast to those seeking to steal, kill, and destroy, there is One who "has come so that they may have life and have it in abundance" (v. 10). Perhaps this isn't the way you often think about God. It's commonly presented that following God's voice is a sure way to lead a boring, legalistic, dull life. But Jesus says that His voice guides His people to the full and abundant life that God wants them to experience. Much like shepherds with sheep, Jesus is wanting to take us to places of joy, peace, and blessing. He's not out to crush our lives, but to give us life.

So we should listen to the voice of the Good Shepherd. If we neglect His voice, we will be like the sheep who strays from the fold. An isolated sheep without a shepherd is a dead sheep. Sooner or later, something is going to come and take that sheep out. The same is true for us. We best remain close to the Shepherd and to His word if we want to avoid peril. And, positively, staying close to Him is the best way to experience life to the fullest. When we train ourselves to hear His word—whether through sermons, through personal reading, through Scripture that the Spirit brings to mind throughout the day—and to obey, we are best positioned to enjoy life under the sun.

How is God speaking to you today?

_____

_____

_____

_____

_____

_____

_____

_____

_____

_____

DAY SIXTY-FIVE

SCRIPTURE READING
Hebrews 11:1-12:2

It's interesting that Solomon ends the book of Ecclesiastes this way: "When all has been heard, the conclusion of the matter is this: fear God and keep His commands" (Ecc. 12:13). The wisest, richest, most powerful man in the world boils it all down to this basic truth. The course to a life well-lived is simple—fear and obey God.

With that reality in mind, read all of Hebrews 11 and the first two verses of Hebrews 12. What do you notice about the people mentioned on this list? What is the connection between those on the list in chapter 11 and the exhortation given in Hebrews 12:1-2?

_____

_____

_____

_____

The author of Hebrews is clear about the purpose of chapter 11. He wants to call attention to those who have lived "by faith" throughout human history. Some of these individuals are predictable—Noah, Abraham, Sarah, Moses. We'd expect to see them on a list like this because of their significant role in the story of Scripture. There are others that we'd not expect to find here because they seemingly played a minor role—Gideon, Barak, Samson, Jephthah. Then there are a host of no-names who are simply known because of their suffering:

> Other people were tortured, not accepting release, so that they might gain a better resurrection. Others experienced mockings and scourgings, as well as bonds and imprisonment. They were stoned, they were sawed in two, they died by the sword, they wandered about in sheepskins, in goatskins, destitute, afflicted, and mistreated. The world was not worthy of them. They wandered in deserts and on mountains, hiding in caves and holes in the ground (Heb. 11:35-38).

What unites each of these people is their faith. They did not live perfect lives, but their lives were lived Godward. In the first verse of chapter 11, the author defines this pattern of life: "Now faith is the reality of what is hoped for, the proof of what is not seen." In other words, those who are commended for their faith in this chapter were people who didn't fixate on this life, but instead lived for God's glory. They resisted the urge to live for what they could see, and instead invested in what they could not see. To borrow Solomon's words from Ecclesiastes, they were people who did not pursue what was under the sun, but chose to give themselves to what lies beyond the sun.

The challenge given in Hebrews 12:1-2 models this pattern of life. The author encourages his readers, and all subsequent Christians, to fixate on Jesus, who modeled perfectly a life of faith. Jesus was intent on pleasing His Father and fulfilling His mission in coming to this earth. He willingly laid aside His position at the right hand of the Father and came to this earth to suffer and die (Phil. 2:1-11). There is no greater example of living for the unseen.

We, too, can live for the unseen realm of God's kingdom. The passage in Hebrews tells us how. We focus our affection and attention on Jesus. We remind ourselves over and over again of His model of self-sacrifice. We accept the pardon for our sins that He purchased for us through His substitutionary death. We consider His pattern of life, and, through the power of the Holy Spirit, we give ourselves to the path of obedience that He desires from us.

It's appropriate, then, for us to finish our journey together by reflecting on faith. Solomon's masterful wisdom found in the book of Ecclesiastes reminds us that nothing under the sun will satisfy the human heart. We've seen the reality of Augustine's famous claim—"Our hearts are restless until they rest in You." Truly, the desires of our heart will never be satisfied with the shiny trinkets offered in this life. God alone can meet the deep longings of our heart.

This doesn't mean we are disinterested or disengaged in the things of this world. As Solomon reminds us, we can find joy in life under the sun when we aren't looking to those things to satisfy our heart. When we find ultimate fulfillment in God, we can then find secondary joy in the good gifts that He provides. Jesus commends such a life goal when He says, "... seek first the kingdom of God and his righteousness, and all these things will be provided for you" (Matt. 6:33). It's no mistake that Solomon ends his book with a call to fear and obey God, and Jesus echos this life-goal in His most famous sermon. Seek God, obey Him, and as you do, trust that He will give you everything else you need for life and godliness.

What steps can you take to actively seek God's kingdom as your first priority?

_____

_____

_____

_____

What concepts or points of application stand out to you as you reflect on the whole of the book of Ecclesiastes?

_____

_____

_____

_____

WEEK THIRTEEN | SIXTY-FIVE

312

WHERE DO I
GO FROM HERE?

One of the secondary goals of *Matters of the Heart* is to cultivate daily Bible reading. Congratulations! You've spent the last 13 weeks engaging with God's word. That's enough time for these patterns to become a habit that we hope will carry over to your daily rhythms going forward.

An easy place to start would be to jump into the book of Proverbs. There are thirty-one chapters in the Proverbs, so you can consider one chapter each day. Solomon is also the author of Proverbs and many of the themes are similar to the book of Ecclesiastes— so it's a natural next step.

Another option would be to work through the book your church is preaching through on Sunday mornings. Often, the pastor will have the book broken down into bite-sized chunks, and you can read and reflect on that passage before or after it's preached. The approach we've taken in this book is to isolate some of the themes mentioned in the passage and consider complementary Scripture that speaks to the theme. You can notice the cross-referenced passages in your Bible and read them as a devotion. Or you can search for that theme online and see what other passages are suggested. Then, use a tool like the 7 Arrows Bible reading plan to help you engage with the passage, understand what it means, and apply it to your life.